The State of Innocence by John Dryden

THE STATE OF INNOCENCE, AND FALL OF MAN.

AN OPERA.

—Utinam modò dicere possem
Carmina digna deâ: Certe est dea carmine digna.
OVID. MET.

John Dryden was born on August 9th, 1631 in the village rectory of Aldwincle near Thrapston in Northamptonshire. As a boy Dryden lived in the nearby village of Titchmarsh, Northamptonshire. In 1644 he was sent to Westminster School as a King's Scholar.

Dryden obtained his BA in 1654, graduating top of the list for Trinity College, Cambridge that year.

Returning to London during The Protectorate, Dryden now obtained work with Cromwell's Secretary of State, John Thurloe.

At Cromwell's funeral on 23 November 1658 Dryden was in the company of the Puritan poets John Milton and Andrew Marvell. The setting was to be a sea change in English history. From Republic to Monarchy and from one set of lauded poets to what would soon become the Age of Dryden.

The start began later that year when Dryden published the first of his great poems, Heroic Stanzas (1658), a eulogy on Cromwell's death.

With the Restoration of the Monarchy in 1660 Dryden celebrated in verse with Astraea Redux, an authentic royalist panegyric.

With the re-opening of the theatres after the Puritan ban, Dryden began to also write plays. His first play, The Wild Gallant, appeared in 1663 but was not successful. From 1668 on he was contracted to produce three plays a year for the King's Company, in which he became a shareholder. During the 1660s and '70s, theatrical writing was his main source of income.

In 1667, he published Annus Mirabilis, a lengthy historical poem which described the English defeat of the Dutch naval fleet and the Great Fire of London in 1666. It established him as the pre-eminent poet of his generation, and was crucial in his attaining the posts of Poet Laureate (1668) and then historiographer royal (1670).

This was truly the Age of Dryden, he was the foremost English Literary figure in Poetry, Plays, translations and other forms.

In 1694 he began work on what would be his most ambitious and defining work as translator, The Works of Virgil (1697), which was published by subscription. It was a national event.

John Dryden died on May 12th, 1700, and was initially buried in St. Anne's cemetery in Soho, before being exhumed and reburied in Westminster Abbey ten days later.

Index of Contents

THE STATE OF INNOCENCE, &c.
TO HER ROYAL HIGHNESS, THE DUCHESS[1].
TO MR DRYDEN, ON HIS POEM OF PARADISE.
THE AUTHOR'S APOLOGY FOR HEROIC POETRY, AND POETIC LICENCE.
THE STATE OF INNOCENCE, AND FALL OF MAN
ACT I
SCENE I
ACT II
SCENE I—A Champaign Country
SCENE II—Paradise
ACT III
SCENE I—Paradise
ACT IV
SCENE I—Paradise
ACT V
SCENE I—Paradise
John Dryden – A Short Biography
John Dryden – A Concise Bibliography

THE STATE OF INNOCENCE, &c.

The "Paradise Lost" of Milton is a work so extraordinary in conception and execution, that it required a lapse of many years to reconcile the herd of readers, and of critics, to what was almost too sublime for ordinary understandings. The poets, in particular, seemed to have gazed on its excellencies, like the inferior animals on Dryden's immortal Hind; and, incapable of fully estimating a merit, which, in some degree, they could not help feeling, many were their absurd experiments to lower it to the standard of their own comprehension. One author, deeming the "Paradise Lost" deficient in harmony, was pleased painfully to turn it into rhyme; and more than one, conceiving the subject too serious to be treated in verse of any kind, employed their leisure in humbling it into prose. The names of these well-judging and considerate persons are preserved by Mr Todd in his edition of Milton's Poetical Works.

But we must not confound with these effusions of gratuitous folly an alteration, or imitation, planned and executed by John Dryden; although we may be at a loss to guess the motives by which he was guided in hazarding such an attempt. His reverence for Milton and his high estimation of his poetry, had already called forth the well-known verses, in which he attributes to him the joint excellencies of the two most celebrated poets of antiquity; and if other proofs of his veneration were wanting, they may be found in the preface to this very production. Had the subject been of a nature which admitted its being actually represented, we might conceive, that Dryden, who was under engagements to the theatre, with which it was not always easy to comply, might have been desirous to shorten his own labour, by adopting the story sentiments, and language of a poem, which he so highly esteemed and which might probably have been new to the generality of his audience. But the costume of our first parents, had there been no other objection, must have excluded the "State of Innocence" from the stage, and accordingly it was certainly never intended for representation. The probable motive, therefore, of this alteration, was the wish, so common to genius, to exert itself upon a subject in which another had already attained brilliant success, or, as Dryden has termed a similar attempt, the desire to shoot in the bow of Ulysses. Some circumstances in the history of Milton's immortal poem may have suggested to Dryden the precise form of the present attempt. It is reported by Voltaire, and seems at length to be admitted, that the original idea of the "Paradise Lost" was supplied by an Italian Mystery, or religious play, which Milton witnessed when abroad[1]; and it is certain, that he intended at first to mould his poem into a dramatic form[2]. It seems, therefore, likely, that Dryden, conscious of his own powers, and enthusiastically admiring those of Milton, was induced to make an experiment upon the forsaken plan of the blind bard, which, with his usual rapidity of conception and execution, he completed in the short space of one month. The spurious copies which got abroad, and perhaps the desire of testifying his respect for his beautiful patroness, the Duchess of York, form his own apology for the publication. It is reported by Mr Aubrey that the step was not taken without Dryden's reverence to Milton being testified by a personal application for his permission. The aged poet, conscious that the might of his versification could receive no addition even from the flowing numbers of Dryden, is stated to have answered with indifference—"Ay, you may tag my verses, if you will."

The structure and diction of this opera, as it is somewhat improperly termed, being rather a dramatic poem, strongly indicate the taste of Charles the Second's reign, for what was ingenious, acute, and polished, in preference to the simplicity of the true sublime. The judgment of that age, as has been already noticed, is always to be referred rather to the head than to the heart; and a poem, written to please mere critics, requires an introduction and display of art, to the exclusion of natural beauty.—This explains the extravagant panegyric of Lee on Dryden's play:

—Milton did the wealthy mine disclose,
And rudely cast what you could well dispose;
He roughly drew, on an old-fashioned ground,
A chaos; for no perfect world was found,
Till through the heap your mighty genius shined:
He was the golden ore, which you refined.
He first beheld the beauteous rustic maid,
And to a place of strength the prize conveyed:
You took her thence; to Court this virgin brought,
Dressed her with gems, new-weaved her hard-spun thought,
And softest language sweetest manners taught;
Till from a comet she a star did rise,
Not to affright, but please, our wondering eyes.

Doubtless there were several critics of that period, who held the heretical opinion above expressed by Lee. And the imitation was such as to warrant that conclusion, considering the school in which it was formed. The scene of the consultation in Pandemonium, and of the soliloquy of Satan on his arrival in the newly-created universe, would possess great merit, did they not unfortunately remind us of the majestic simplicity of Milton. But there is often a sort of Ovidian point in the diction which seems misplaced. Thus, Asmodeus tells us, that the devils, ascending from the lake of fire,

Shake off their slumber first, and next their fear.

And, with Dryden's usual hate to the poor Dutchmen, the council of Pandemonium are termed,

Most High and Mighty Lords, who better fell
From heaven, to rise States General of hell.

There is one inconvenience, which, as this poem was intended for perusal only, the author, one would have thought, might have easily avoided. This arises from the stage directions, which supply the place of the terrific and beautiful descriptions of Milton. What idea, except burlesque, can we form of the expulsion of the fallen angels from heaven, literally represented by their tumbling down upon the stage? or what feelings of terror can be excited by the idea of an opera hell, composed of pasteboard and flaming rosin? If these follies were not actually to be produced before our eyes, it could serve no good purpose to excite the image of them in our imaginations. They are circumstances by which we feel, that scenic deception must be rendered ridiculous; and ought to be avoided, even in a drama intended for perusal only, since they cannot be mentioned without exciting ludicrous combinations.—Even in describing the primitive state of our first parents, Dryden has displayed some of the false and corrupted taste of the court of Charles. Eve does not consent to her union with Adam without coquettish apprehensions of his infidelity, which circumstances rendered rather improbable; and even in the state of innocence, she avows the love of sway and of self, which, in a loose age, is thought the principal attribute of her daughters. It may be remembered that the Adam of Milton, when first experiencing the powers of slumber, thought,

I then was passing to my former state
Insensible, and forthwith to dissolve.

The Eve of Dryden expresses the same apprehensions of annihilation upon a very different occasion. These passages form a contrast highly favourable to the simplicity and chastity of Milton's taste. The school logic, employed by Adam and the angels in the first scene of the fourth act, however misplaced, may be paralleled if not justified, by similar instances in the "Paradise Lost."

On the other hand, the "State of Innocence" contains many passages of varied and happy expression peculiar to our great poet; and the speech of Lucfier in Paradise (Act third, scene first), approaches in sublimity to his prototype in Milton, Indeed, altered as this poem was from the original, in order to accommodate it to the taste of a frivolous age, it still retained too much fancy to escape the raillery of the men of wit and fashion, more disposed to "laugh at extravagance, than to sympathise with feelings of grandeur." The "Companion to the Theatre" mentions an objection started by the more nice and delicate critics, against the anachronism and absurdity of Lucifer conversing about the world, its form and vicissitudes, at a time previous to its creation, or, at least, to the possibility of his knowing any thing of it. But to this objection, which applies to the "Paradise Lost" also, it is sufficient to reply, that the measure of intelligence, competent to supernatural beings, being altogether unknown to us, leaves the poet at liberty to accommodate its extent to the purposes in which he employs them, without which poetic license, it would be in vain to introduce them. Dryden, moved by this, and similar objections, has prefixed to the drama, "An Apology for Heroic Poetry," and the use of what is technically called "the machinery" employed in it.

Upon the whole, it may be justly questioned, whether Dryden shewed his judgment in the choice of a subject which compelled an immediate parallel betwixt Milton and himself, upon a subject so exclusively favourable to the powers of the former. Indeed, according to Dennis, notwithstanding Dryden's admiration of Milton, he evinced sufficiently by this undertaking, what he himself confessed twenty years afterwards, that he was not sensible of half the extent of his excellence. In the "Town and Country Mouse," Mr Bayes is made to term Milton "a rough unhewen fellow;" and Dryden himself, even in the dedication to the Translation from Juvenal, a work of his advanced life, alleges, that, though he found in that poet a true sublimity, and lofty thoughts, clothed with admirable Grecisms, he did not find the elegant turn of words and expression proper to the Italian poets and to Spenser. In the same treatise, he undertakes to excuse, but not to justify Milton, for his choice of blank verse, affirming that he possessed neither grace nor facility in rhyming. A consciousness of the harmony of his own numbers, and a predilection for that kind of verse, in which he excelled, seemed to have encouraged him to think he could improve the "Paradise Lost." Baker observes but too truly, that the "State of Innocence" recals the idea reprobated by Marvell in his address to Milton:

Or if a work so infinite be spanned,
Jealous I was, lest some less skilful hand,
Such as disquiet always what is well,
And by ill-imitating would excel,
Might hence presume the whole creation's day
To change in scenes, and shew it in a play.

The "State of Innocence" seems to have been undertaken by Dryden during a cessation of his theatrical labours, and was first published in 1674, shortly after the death of Milton, which took place on the 8th of November in the same year.

Footnotes

1. The Adamo of Andreini; for an account of which, see Todd's Milton, Vol. I. the elegant Hayley's Conjectures on the Origin of Paradise Lost, and Walker's Memoir on Italian Tragedy. The Drama of Andreini opens with a grand chorus of angels, who sing to this purpose:

Let the rainbow be the fiddle-stick to the fiddle of heaven,
Let the spheres be the strings, and the stars the musical notes;
Let the new-born breezes make the pauses and sharps,
And let time be careful to beat the measure.

2. See a sketch of his plan in Johnson's Life of Milton, and in the authorities above quoted.

TO HER ROYAL HIGHNESS, THE DUCHESS[1].

MADAM,

Ambition is so far from being a vice in poets, that it is almost impossible for them to succeed without it. Imagination must be raised, by a desire of fame, to a desire of pleasing; and they whom, in all ages, poets have endeavoured most to please, have been the beautiful and the great. Beauty is their deity, to which they sacrifice, and greatness is their guardian angel, which protects them. Both these, are so eminently joined in the person of your royal highness, that it were not easy for any but a poet to determine which of them outshines the other. But I confess, madam, I am already biassed in my choice. I can easily resign to others the praise of your illustrious family, and that glory which you derive from a long-continued race of princes, famous for their actions both in peace and war: I can give up, to the historians of your country, the names of so many generals and heroes which crowd their annals, and to our own the hopes of those which you are to produce for the British chronicle. I can yield, without envy, to the nation of poets, the family of Este, to which Ariosto and Tasso have owed their patronage, and to which the world has owed their poems. But I could not, without extreme reluctance, resign the theme of your beauty to another hand. Give me leave, madam, to acquaint the world, that I am jealous of this subject; and let it be no dishonour to you, that, after having raised the admiration of mankind, you have inspired one man to give it voice. But, with whatsoever vanity this new honour of being your poet has filled my mind, I confess myself too weak for the inspiration: the priest was always unequal to the oracle: the god within him was too mighty for his breast: he laboured with the sacred revelation, and there was more of the mystery left behind, than the divinity itself could enable him to express. I can but discover a part of your excellencies to the world; and that, too, according to the measure of my own weakness. Like those who have surveyed the moon by glasses, I can only tell of a new and shining world above us, but not relate the riches and glories of the place. 'Tis therefore that I have already waved the subject of your greatness, to resign myself to the contemplation of what is more peculiarly yours. Greatness is indeed communicated to some few of both sexes; but beauty is confined to a more narrow compass: 'tis only in your sex, 'tis not shared by many, and its supreme perfection is in you alone. And here, madam, I am proud that I cannot flatter; you have reconciled the differing judgments of mankind; for all men are equal in their judgment of what is eminently best. The prize of beauty was disputed only till you were seen; but now all pretenders have withdrawn their claims: there is no competition but for the second place; even the fairest of our island, which is famed for beauties, not daring to commit their cause against you to the suffrage of those, who most partially adore them. Fortune has, indeed, but rendered justice to so much excellence, in setting it so high to public view; or, rather, Providence has done justice to itself, in placing the most perfect workmanship of heaven, where it may be admired by all beholders. Had the sun and stars been seated lower, their glory had not been communicated to all at once, and the Creator had wanted so much of his praise, as he had made your condition more obscure: but he has placed you so near a crown, that you add a lustre to it by your beauty. You are joined to a prince, who only could deserve you; whose conduct, courage, and success in war; whose fidelity to his royal brother, whose love for his country, whose constancy to his friends, whose bounty to his servants, whose justice to merit, whose inviolable truth, and whose magnanimity in all his actions, seem to have been rewarded by heaven by the gift of you. You are never seen but you are blest; and I am sure you bless all those who see you. We think not the day is long enough when we behold you; and you are so much the business of our souls, that while you are in sight, we can neither look nor think on any else. There are no eyes for other beauties; you only are present, and the rest of your sex are but the unregarded parts that fill your triumph. Our sight is so intent on the object of its admiration, that our tongues have not leisure even to praise you: for language seems too low a thing to express your excellence; and our souls are speaking so much within, that they despise all foreign conversation. Every man, even the dullest, is thinking more than the most eloquent can teach him how to utter. Thus, madam, in the midst of crowds, you reign in solitude; and are adored with the deepest veneration, that of silence. 'Tis true, you are above all mortal wishes; no man desires impossibilities, because they are beyond the reach of nature. To hope to be a god, is folly exalted into madness; but, by the laws of our creation, we are obliged to adore him, and are permitted to love him too at human distance. 'Tis the nature of perfection to be attractive, but the excellency of the object refines the nature of the love. It strikes an impression of awful reverence; 'tis indeed that love which is more properly a zeal than passion. 'Tis the rapture which anchorites find in prayer, when a beam of the divinity shines upon them; that which makes them despise all worldly objects; and yet 'tis all but contemplation. They are seldom visited from above, but a single vision so transports them, that it makes up the happiness of their lives. Mortality cannot bear it often: it finds them in the eagerness and height of their devotion; they are speechless for the time that it continues, and prostrate and dead when it departs. That ecstacy had need be strong, which, without any end, but that of admiration has power enough to destroy all other passions. You render mankind insensible to other beauties, and have destroyed the empire of love in a court which was the seat of his dominion. You have subverted (may I dare to accuse you of it?) even our fundamental laws; and reign absolute over the hearts of a stubborn and free-born people, tenacious almost to madness of their liberty. The brightest and most victorious of our ladies make daily complaints of revolted subjects, if they may be said to be revolted, whose servitude is not accepted; for your royal highness is too great, and too just a monarch, either to want or to receive the homage of rebellious fugitives. Yet, if some few among the multitude continue stedfast to their first pretensions, 'tis an obedience so lukewarm and languishing, that it merits not the name of passion; their addresses are so faint, and their vows so hollow to their sovereigns, that they seem only to maintain their faith out of a sense of honour: they are ashamed to desist, and yet grow careless to obtain. Like despairing combatants, they strive against you as if they had beheld unveiled the magical shield of your Ariosto, which dazzled the beholders with too much brightness. They can no longer hold up their arms; they have read their destiny in your eyes:

Splende lo scudo, a guisa di piropo;
E luce altra non é tanto lucente:
Cader in terra a lo splendor fu d'vopo,
Con gli occhi abbacinati, e senza mente.

And yet, madam, if I could find in myself the power to leave this argument of your incomparable beauty, I might turn to one which would equally oppress me with its greatness; for your conjugal virtues have deserved to be set as an example, to a less degenerate, less tainted age. They approach so near to singularity in ours, that I can scarcely make a panegyric to your royal highness, without a satire on many others. But your person is a paradise, and your soul a cherubim within, to guard it. If the excellence of the outside invite the beholders, the majesty of your mind deters them from too bold approaches, and turns their admiration into religion. Moral perfections are raised higher by you in the softer sex; as if men were of too coarse a mould for heaven to work on, and that the image of divinity could not be cast to likeness in so harsh a metal. Your person is so admirable, that it can scarce receive addition, when it shall be glorified: and your soul, which shines through it, finds it of a substance so near her own, that she will be pleased to pass an age within it, and to be confined to such a palace.

I know not how I am hurried back to my former theme; I ought and purposed to have celebrated those endowments and qualities of your mind, which were sufficient, even without the graces of your person, to render you, as you are, the ornament of the court, and the object of wonder to three kingdoms. But all my praises are but as a bull-rush cast upon a stream; if they sink not, 'tis because they are borne up by the strength of the current, which supports their lightness; but they are carried round again, and return on the eddy where they first began. I can proceed no farther than your beauty; and even on that too I have said so little, considering the greatness of the subject, that, like him who would lodge a bowl upon a precipice, either my praise falls back, by the weakness of the delivery, or stays not on the top, but rolls over, and is lost on the other side. I intended this a dedication; but how can I consider what belongs to myself, when I have been so long contemplating on you! Be pleased then, madam, to receive this poem, without entitling so much excellency as yours, to the faults and imperfections of so mean a writer; and instead of being favourable to the piece, which merits nothing, forgive the presumption of the author; who is, with all possible veneration,

Your Royal Highness's
Most obedient, most humble,
Most devoted servant,
JOHN DRYDEN.

Footnote

1. Mary of Este, daughter of the Duke of Modena, and second wife to James Duke of York, afterwards James II. She was married to him by proxy in 1673, and came over in the year following. Notwithstanding her husband's unpopularity, and her own attachment to the Roman Catholic religion, her youth, beauty, and innocence secured her from insult and slander during all the stormy period which preceded her accession to the crown. Even Burnet, reluctantly, admits the force of her charms, and the inoffensiveness of her conduct. But her beauty produced a more lasting effect on the young and gallant, than on that austere and stubborn partizan; and its force must be allowed, since it was extolled even when Mary was dethroned and exiled. Granville, Lord Lansdowne, has praised her in "The Progress of Beauty;" and I cannot forbear transcribing some of the verses, on account of the gallant spirit of the author, who scorned to change with fortune, and continued to admire and celebrate, in adversity, the charms which he had worshipped in the meridian of prosperity.

And now, my muse, a nobler flight prepare,
And sing so loud, that heaven and earth may hear.
Behold from Italy an awful ray
Of heavenly light illuminates the day;
Northward she bends, majestically bright,
And here she fixes her imperial light.
Be bold, be bold, my muse, nor fear to raise
Thy voice to her who was thy earliest praise[a].
What though the sullen fates refuse to shine,
Or frown severe on thy audacious line;
Keep thy bright theme within thy steady sight,
The clouds shall fly before thy dazzling light,
And everlasting day direct thy lofty flight.
Thou, who hast never yet put on disguise,
To flatter faction, or descend to vice,
Let no vain fear thy generous ardour tame,
But stand erect, and sound as loud as fame.
As when our eye some prospect would pursue,
Descending from a hill looks round to view,
Passes o'er lawns and meadows, till it gains
Some favourite spot, and fixing there remains;
With equal ardour my transported muse
Flies other objects, this bright theme to chuse.
Queen of our hearts, and charmer of our sight!
A monarch's pride, his glory and delight!
Princess adored and loved! if verse can give
A deathless name, thine shall for ever live;

Invoked where'er the British lion roars,
Extended as the seas that guard the British shores.
The wise immortals, in their seats above,
To crown their labours still appointed love;
Phoebus enjoyed the goddess of the sea,
Alcides had Omphale, James has thee.
O happy James! content thy mighty mind,
Grudge not the world, for still thy queen is kind;
To be but at whose feet more glory brings,
Than 'tis to tread on sceptres and on kings.
Secure of empire in that beauteous breast,
Who would not give their crowns to be so blest?
Was Helen half so fair, so formed for joy,
Well chose the Trojan, and well burned was Troy.
But ah! what strange vicissitudes of fate,
What chance attends on every worldly state!
As when the skies were sacked, the conquered gods,
Compelled from heaven, forsook their blessed abodes;
Wandering in woods, they hid from den to den,
And sought their safety in the shapes of men;
As when the winds with kindling flames conspire,
The blaze increases as they fan the fire;
From roof to roof the burning torrent pours,
Nor spares the palace nor the loftiest towers;
Or as the stately pine, erecting high
Her lofty branches shooting to the sky,
If riven by the thunderbolt of Jove,
Down falls at once the pride of all the grove;
Level with lowest shrubs lies the tall head,
That, reared aloft, as to the clouds was spread,
So—
But cease, my muse, thy colours are too faint;
Shade with a veil those griefs thou can'st not paint.
That sun is set!—

Progress of Beauty.

The beauty, which inspired the romantic and unchanging admiration of Granville, may be allowed to justify some of the flights of Dryden's panegyric. I fear enough will still remain to justify the stricture of Johnson, who observes, that Dryden's dedication is an "attempt to mingle earth and heaven, by praising human excellence in the language of religion."

At the date of this address, the Duchess of York was only in her sixteenth year.

Footnote

a. He had written verses to the Earl of Peterborough, on the Duke of York's marriage with the Princess of Modena, before he was twelve years old.

TO MR DRYDEN, ON HIS POEM OF PARADISE.

Forgive me, awful poet, if a muse,
Whom artless nature did for plainness chuse,
In loose attire presents her humble thought,
Of this best poem that you ever wrought.
This fairest labour of your teeming brain
I would embrace, but not with flatt'ry stain.
Something I would to your vast virtue raise,
But scorn to daub it with a fulsome praise;
That would but blot the work I would commend,
And shew a court-admirer, not a friend.
To the dead bard your fame a little owes,
For Milton did the wealthy mine disclose,
And rudely cast what you could well dispose:
He roughly drew, on an old fashioned ground,
A chaos; for no perfect world was found,
Till through the heap your mighty genius shined:
He was the golden ore, which you refined.
He first beheld the beauteous rustic maid,
And to a place of strength the prize conveyed:
You took her thence; to court this virgin brought,
Drest her with gems, new weaved her hard-spun thought,
And softest language sweetest manners taught;
Till from a comet she a star doth rise,
Not to affright, but please, our wondering eyes.
Betwixt you both is trained a nobler piece,
Than e'er was drawn in Italy or Greece.
Thou from his source of thoughts even souls dost bring,
As smiling gods from sullen Saturn spring.
When night's dull mask the face of heaven does wear,
'Tis doubtful light, but here and there a star,
Which serves the dreadful shadows to display,
That vanish at the rising of the day;
But then bright robes the meadows all adorn,
And the world looks as it were newly born.
So, when your sense his mystic reason cleared,
The melancholy scene all gay appeared;
Now light leapt up, and a new glory smiled,
And all throughout was mighty, all was mild.
Before this palace, which thy wit did build,
Which various fancy did so gaudy gild,
And judgment has with solid riches filled,
My humbler muse begs she may sentry stand,
Amongst the rest that guard this Eden land.

But there's no need, for ev'n thy foes conspire
Thy praise, and, hating thee, thy work admire.
On then, O mightiest of the inspired men!
Monarch of verse! new themes employ thy pen.
The troubles of majestic Charles set down;
Not David vanquished more to reach a crown.
Praise him as Cowley did that Hebrew king:
Thy theme's as great; do thou as greatly sing.
Then thou may'st boldly to his favour rise,
Look down, and the base serpent's hiss despise;
From thund'ring envy safe in laurel sit,
While clam'rous critics their vile heads submit,
Condemned for treason at the bar of wit.

NAT. LEE.

THE AUTHOR'S APOLOGY FOR HEROIC POETRY, AND POETIC LICENCE.

To satisfy the curiosity of those, who will give themselves the trouble of reading the ensuing poem, I think myself obliged to render them a reason why I publish an opera which was never acted. In the first place, I shall not be ashamed to own, that my chiefest motive was, the ambition which I acknowledged in the Epistle. I was desirous to lay at the feet of so beautiful and excellent a princess, a work, which, I confess, was unworthy her, but which, I hope, she will have the goodness to forgive. I was also induced to it in my own defence; many hundred copies of it being dispersed abroad without my knowledge, or consent: so that every one gathering new faults, it became at length a libel against me; and I saw, with some disdain, more nonsense than either I, or as bad a poet, could have crammed into it, at a month's warning; in which time it was wholly written, and not since revised. After this, I cannot, without injury to the deceased author of "Paradise Lost," but acknowledge, that this poem has received its entire foundation, part of the design, and many of the ornaments, from him. What I have borrowed will be so easily discerned from my mean productions, that I shall not need to point the reader to the places: And truly I should be sorry, for my own sake, that any one should take the pains to compare them together; the original being undoubtedly one of the greatest, most noble, and most sublime poems, which either this age or nation has produced. And though I could not refuse the partiality of my friend, who is pleased to commend me in his verses, I hope they will rather be esteemed the effect of his love to me, than of his deliberate and sober judgment. His genius is able to make beautiful what he pleases: Yet, as he has been too favourable to me, I doubt not but he will hear of his kindness from many of our contemporaries for we are fallen into an age of illiterate, censorious, and detracting people, who, thus qualified, set up for critics.

In the first place, I must take leave to tell them, that they wholly mistake the nature of criticism, who think its business is principally to find fault. Criticism, as it was first instituted by Aristotle, was meant a standard of judging well; the chiefest part of which is, to observe those excellencies which should delight a reasonable reader. If the design, the conduct, the thoughts, and the expressions of a poem, be generally such as proceed from a true genius of poetry, the critic ought to pass his judgement in favour of the author. It is malicious and unmanly to snarl at the little lapses of a pen, from which Virgil himself stands not exempted. Horace acknowledges, that honest Homer nods sometimes: He is not equally awake in every line; but he leaves it also as a standing measure for our judgments,

—Non, ubi plura nitent in carmine, paucis
Offendi maculis, quas aut incuria fudit,
Aut humana parùm cavit natura.—

And Longinus, who was undoubtedly, after Aristotle the greatest critic amongst the Greeks, in his twenty-seventh chapter, [Greek: PERI HUPSOUS], has judiciously preferred the sublime genius that sometimes errs, to the middling or indifferent one, which makes few faults, but seldom or never rises to any excellence. He compares the first to a man of large possessions, who has not leisure to consider of every slight expence, will not debase himself to the management of every trifle: Particular sums are not laid out, or spared, to the greatest advantage in his economy; but are sometimes suffered to run to waste, while he is only careful of the main. On the other side, he likens the mediocrity of wit, to one of a mean fortune, who manages his store with extreme frugality, or rather parsimony; but who, with fear of running into profuseness, never arrives to the magnificence of living. This kind of genius writes indeed correctly. A wary man he is in grammar, very nice as to solecism or barbarism, judges to a hair of little decencies, knows better than any man what is not to be written, and never hazards himself so far as to fall, but plods on deliberately, and, as a grave man ought, is sure to put his staff before him. In short, he sets his heart upon it, and with wonderful care makes his business sure; that is, in plain English, neither to be blamed nor praised.—I could, says my author, find out some blemishes in Homer; and am perhaps as naturally inclined to be disgusted at a fault as another man; but, after all, to speak impartially, his failings are such, as are only marks of human frailty: they are little mistakes, or rather negligences, which have escaped his pen in the fervour of his writing; the sublimity of his spirit carries it with me against his carelessness; and though Apollonius his "Argonauts," and Theocritus his "Idyllia," are more free from errors, there is not any man of so false a judgment, who would chuse rather to have been Apollonius or Theocritus, than Homer.

It is worth our consideration a little, to examine how much these hypercritics in English poetry differ from the opinion of the Greek and Latin judges of antiquity; from the Italians and French, who have succeeded them; and, indeed, from the general taste and approbation of all ages. Heroic poetry, which they condemn, has ever been esteemed, and ever will be, the greatest work of human nature: In that rank has Aristotle placed it; and Longinus is so full of the like expressions, that he abundantly confirms the other's testimony. Horace as plainly delivers his opinion, and particularly praises Homer in these verses:

Trojani Belli scriptorem, maxime Lolli,
Dum tu declamas Romæ, Præneste relegi:
Qui quid sit pulchrum, quid turpe, quid utile, quid non,
Plenius ac melius Chrysippo et Crantore dicit.

And in another place, modestly excluding himself from the number of poets, because he only writ odes and satires, he tells you a poet is such an one,

—Cui mens divinior, atque os
Magna soniturum.

Quotations are superfluous in an established truth; otherwise I could reckon up, amongst the moderns, all the Italian commentators on Aristotle's book of poetry; and, amongst the French, the greatest of this age, Boileau and Rapin; the latter of which is alone sufficient, were all other critics lost, to teach anew the rules of writing. Any man, who will seriously consider the nature of an epic poem, how it agrees with that of poetry in general, which is to instruct and to delight, what actions it describes, and what persons they are chiefly whom it informs, will find it a work which indeed is full of difficulty in the attempt, but admirable when it is well performed. I write not this with the least intention to undervalue the other parts of poetry: for Comedy is both excellently instructive, and extremely pleasant; satire lashes vice into reformation, and humour represents folly so as to render it ridiculous. Many of our present writers are eminent in both these kinds; and, particularly, the author of the "Plain Dealer," whom I am proud to call my friend, has obliged all honest and virtuous men, by one of the most bold, most general, and most useful satires, which has ever been presented on the English theatre. I do not dispute the preference of Tragedy; let every man enjoy his taste: but it is unjust, that they, who have not the least notion of heroic writing, should therefore condemn the pleasure which others receive from it, because they cannot comprehend it. Let them please their appetites in eating what they like; but let them not force their dish on all the table. They, who would combat general authority with particular opinion, must first establish themselves a reputation of understanding better than other men. Are all the flights of heroic poetry to be concluded bombast, unnatural, and mere madness, because they are not affected with their excellencies? It is just as reasonable as to conclude there is no day, because a blind man cannot distinguish of light and colours. Ought they not rather, in modesty, to doubt of their own judgments, when they think this or that expression in Homer, Virgil, Tasso, or Milton's "Paradise," to be too far strained, than positively to conclude, that it is all fustian, and mere nonsense? It is true, there are limits to be set betwixt the boldness and rashness of a poet; but he must understand those limits, who pretends to judge as well as he who undertakes to write: and he who has no liking to the whole, ought, in reason, to be excluded from censuring of the parts. He must be a lawyer before he mounts the tribunal; and the judicature of one court, too, does not qualify a man to preside in another. He may be an excellent pleader in the Chancery, who is not fit to rule the Common Pleas. But I will presume for once to tell them, that the boldest strokes of poetry, when they are managed artfully, are those which most delight the reader.

Virgil and Horace, the severest writers of the severest age, have made frequent use of the hardest metaphors, and of the strongest hyperboles; and in this case the best authority is the best argument; for generally to have pleased, and through all ages, must bear the force of universal tradition. And if you would appeal from thence to right reason, you will gain no more by it in effect, than, first, to set up your reason against those authors; and, secondly, against all those who have admired them. You must prove, why that ought not to have pleased, which has pleased the most learned, and the most judicious; and, to be thought knowing, you must first put the fool upon all mankind. If you can enter more deeply, than they have done, into the causes and resorts of that which moves pleasure in a reader, the field is open, you may be heard: But those springs of human nature are not so easily discovered by every superficial judge: It requires philosophy, as well as poetry, to sound the depth of all the passions; what they are in themselves, and how they are to be provoked: And in this science the best poets have excelled. Aristotle raised the fabric of his poetry from observation of those things, in which Euripides, Sophocles, and Æschylus pleased: He considered how they raised the passions, and thence has drawn rules for our imitation. From hence have sprung the tropes and figures, for which they wanted a name, who first practised them, and succeeded in them. Thus I grant you, that the knowledge of nature was the original rule; and that all poets ought to study her, as well as Aristotle and Horace, her interpreters. But then this also undeniably follows, that those things, which delight all ages, must have been an imitation of nature; which is all I contend. Therefore is rhetoric made an art; therefore the names of so many tropes and figures were invented; because it was observed they had such and such effect upon the audience. Therefore catachreses and hyperboles have found their place amongst them; not that they were to be avoided, but to be used judiciously, and placed in poetry, as heightenings and shadows are in painting, to make the figure bolder, and cause it to stand off to sight.

Nec retia cervis
Ulla dolum meditantur;

says Virgil in his Eclogues: and speaking of Leander, in his Georgics,

Nocte natat cæca serus freta, quem super ingens
Porta tonat cæli, et scopulis illisa reclamant
Æquora:

In both of these, you see, he fears not to give voice and thought to things inanimate.

Will you arraign your master, Horace, for his hardness of expression, when he describes the death of Cleopatra, and says she did—asperos tractare serpentes, ut atrum corpore combiberet cenenum,—because the body, in that action, performs what is proper to the mouth?

As for hyperboles, I will neither quote Lucan, nor Statius, men of an unbounded imagination, but who often wanted the poize of judgment. The divine Virgil was not liable to that exception; and yet he describes Polyphemus thus:

—Graditurque per æquor
Jam medium; necdum fluctus latera ardua tinxit.

In imitation of this place, our admirable Cowley thus paints Goliah:

The valley, now, this monster seemed to fill;
And we, methought, looked up to him from our hill:

where the two words, seemed and methought, have mollified the figure; and yet if they had not been there, the fright of the Israelites might have excused their belief of the giant's stature[1].

In the eighth of the Æneids, Virgil paints the swiftness of Camilla thus:

Ilia vel intactæ segetis per summa volaret
Gramina, nec teneras cursu læsisset aristas;
Vel mare per medium, fluctu suspensa tumenti,
Ferret iter, celeres nec tingeret æquore plantas.

You are not obliged, as in history, to a literal belief of what the poet says; but you are pleased with the image, without being cozened by the fiction.

Yet even in history, Longinus quotes Herodotus on this occasion of hyperboles. The Lacedemonians, says he, at the straits of Thermopylæ, defended themselves to the last extremity; and when their arms failed them, fought it out with their nails and teeth; till at length, (the Persians shooting continually upon them) they lay buried under the arrows of their enemies. It is not reasonable, (continues the critic) to believe, that men could defend themselves with their nails and teeth from an armed multitude; nor that they lay buried under a pile of darts and arrows; and yet there wants not probability for the figure: because the hyperbole seems not to have been made for the sake of the description; but rather to have been produced from the occasion.

It is true, the boldness of the figures is to be hidden sometimes by the address of the poet; that they may work their effect upon the mind, without discovering the art which caused it. And therefore they are principally to be used in passion; when we speak more warmly, and with more precipitation than at other times: For then, Si vis me flere, dolendum est primum ipsi tibi; the poet must put on the passion he endeavours to represent: A man in such an occasion is not cool enough, either to reason rightly, or to talk calmly. Aggravations are then in their proper places; interrogations, exclamations, hyperbata, or a disordered connection of discourse, are graceful there, because they are natural. The sum of all depends on what before I hinted, that this boldness of expression is not to be blamed, if it be managed by the coolness and discretion which is necessary to a poet.

Yet before I leave this subject, I cannot but take notice how disingenuous our adversaries appear: All that is dull, insipid, languishing, and without sinews, in a poem, they call an imitation of nature: They only offend our most equitable judges, who think beyond them; and lively images and elocution are never to be forgiven.

What fustian, as they call it, have I heard these gentlemen find out in Mr Cowley's Odes! I acknowledge myself unworthy to defend so excellent an author, neither have I room to do it here; only in general I will say, that nothing can appear more beautiful to me, than the strength of those images which they condemn.

Imaging is, in itself, the very height and life of poetry. It is, as Longinus describes it, a discourse, which, by a kind of enthusiasm, or extraordinary emotion of the soul, makes it seem to us, that we behold those things which the poet paints, so as to be pleased with them, and to admire them.

If poetry be imitation, that part of it must needs be best, which describes most lively our actions and passions; our virtues and our vices; our follies and our humours: For neither is comedy without its part of imaging; and they who do it best are certainly the most excellent in their kind. This is too plainly proved to be denied: But how are poetical fictions, how are hippocentaurs and chimeras, or how are angels and immaterial substances to be imaged; which, some of them, are things quite out of nature; others, such whereof we can have no notion? This is the last refuge of our adversaries; and more than any of them have yet had the wit to object against us. The answer is easy to the first part of it: The fiction of some beings which are not in nature, (second notions, as the logicians call them) has been founded on the conjunction of two natures, which have a real separate being. So hippocentaurs were imaged, by joining the natures of a man and horse together; as Lucretius tells us, who has used this word of image oftener than any of the poets:

Nam certè ex vivo centauri non fit imago,
Nulla fuit quoniam talis natura animai:
Verùm ubi equi atque hominis, casu, convenit imago,
Hærescit facilè extemplò, &c.

The same reason may also be alleged for chimeras and the rest. And poets may be allowed the like liberty, for describing things which really exist not, if they are founded on popular belief. Of this nature are fairies, pigmies, and the extraordinary effects of magic; for it is still an imitation, though of other men's fancies: and thus are Shakespeare's "Tempest," his "Midsummer Night's Dream," and Ben Jonson's "Masque of Witches" to be defended. For immaterial substances, we are authorised by Scripture in their description: and herein the text accommodates itself to vulgar apprehension, in giving angels the likeness of beautiful young men. Thus, after the pagan divinity, has Homer drawn his gods with human faces: and thus we have notions of things above us, by describing them like other beings more within our knowledge.

I wish I could produce any one example of excellent imaging in all this poem. Perhaps I cannot; but that which comes nearest it, is in these four lines, which have been sufficiently canvassed by my well-natured censors:

Seraph and cherub, careless of their charge,
And wanton, in full ease now live at large:
Unguarded leave the passes of the sky,
And all dissolved in hallelujahs lie.

I have heard (says one of them) of anchovies dissolved in sauce; but never of an angel in hallelujahs. A mighty witticism! (if you will pardon a new word,) but there is some difference between a laugher and a critic. He might have burlesqued Virgil too, from whom I took the image. Invadunt urbem, somno vinoque sepultam. A city's being buried, is just as proper on occasion, as an angel's being dissolved in ease, and songs of triumph. Mr Cowley lies as open too in many places:

Where their vast courts the mother waters keep, &c.

For if the mass of waters be the mothers, then their daughters, the little streams, are bound, in all good manners, to make courtesy to them, and ask them blessing. How easy it is to turn into ridicule the best descriptions, when once a man is in the humour of laughing, till he wheezes at his own dull jest! but an image, which is strongly and beautifully set before the eyes of the reader, will still be poetry, when the merry fit is over, and last when the other is forgotten.

I promised to say somewhat of Poetic Licence, but have in part anticipated my discourse already. Poetic Licence, I take to be the liberty which poets have assumed to themselves, in all ages, of speaking things in verse, which are beyond the severity of prose. It is that particular character, which distinguishes and sets the bounds betwixt oratio soluta, and poetry. This, as to what regards the thought, or imagination of a poet, consists in fiction: but then those thoughts must be expressed; and here arise two other branches of it; for if this licence be included in a single word, it admits of tropes; if in a sentence or proposition, of figures; both which are of a much larger extent, and more forcibly to be used in verse than prose. This is that birth-right which is derived to us from our great forefathers, even from Homer down to Ben; and they, who would deny it to us, have, in plain terms, the fox's quarrel to the grapes—they cannot reach it.

How far these liberties are to be extended, I will not presume to determine here, since Horace does not. But it is certain that they are to be varied, according to the language and age in which an author writes. That which would be allowed to a Grecian poet, Martial tells you, would not be suffered in a Roman; and it is evident, that the English does more nearly follow the strictness of the latter, than the freedoms of the former. Connection of epithets, or the conjunction of two words in one, are frequent and elegant in the Greek, which yet Sir Philip Sidney, and the translator of Du Bartas, have unluckily attempted in the English; though this, I confess, is not so proper an instance of poetic licence, as it is of variety of idiom in languages.

Horace a little explains himself on this subject of Licentia Poetica, in these verses:

—Pictoribus atque Poetis
Quidlibet audendi semper fuit æqua potestas: ...
Sed non, ut placidis coeant immitia, non ut
Serpentes avibus geminentur, tigribus hædi.

He would have a poem of a piece; not to begin with one thing, and end with another: He restrains it so far, that thoughts of an unlike nature ought not to be joined together. That were indeed to make a chaos. He taxed not Homer, nor the divine Virgil, for interesting their gods in the wars of Troy and Italy; neither, had he now lived, would he have taxed Milton, as our false critics have presumed to do, for his choice of a supernatural argument; but he would have blamed my author, who was a Christian, had he introduced into his poem heathen deities, as Tasso is condemned by Rapin on the like occasion; and as Camoëns, the author of the "Lusiads," ought to be censured by all his readers, when he brings in Bacchus and Christ into the same adventure of his fable.

From that which has been said, it may be collected, that the definition of wit (which has been so often attempted, and ever unsuccessfully by many poets,) is only this: That it is a propriety of thoughts and words; or, in other terms, thoughts and words elegantly adapted to the subject. If our critics will join issue on this definition, that we may convenire in aliquo tertio; if they will take it as a granted principle, it will be easy to put an end to this dispute. No man will disagree from another's judgment concerning the dignity of style in heroic poetry; but all reasonable men will conclude it necessary, that sublime subjects ought to be adorned with the sublimest, and consequently often, with the most figurative expressions. In the mean time I will not run into their fault of imposing my opinions on other men, any more than I would my writings on their taste: I have only laid down, and that superficially enough, my present thoughts; and shall be glad to be taught better by those who pretend to reform our poetry.

Footnote

1. With all this mitigation, the passage seems horrible bombast.

THE STATE OF INNOCENCE, AND FALL OF MAN

ACT I

SCENE I

Represents a Chaos, or a confused Mass of Matter; the Stage is almost wholly dark: A Symphony of warlike Music is heard for some time; then from the Heavens, (which are opened) fall the rebellious

Angels, wheeling in Air, and seeming transfixed with Thunderbolts: The bottom of the Stage being opened, receives the Angels, who fall out of sight. Tunes of Victory are played, and an Hymn sung; Angels discovered above, brandishing their Swords: The Music ceasing, and the Heavens being closed, the Scene shifts, and on a sudden represents Hell: Part of the Scene is a Lake of Brimstone, or rolling Fire; the Earth of a burnt Colour: The fallen Angels appear on the Lake, lying prostrate; a Tune of Horror and Lamentation is heard.

[LUCIFER, raising himself on the Lake.

LUCIFER
Is this the seat our conqueror has given?
And this the climate we must change for heaven?
These regions and this realm my wars have got;
This mournful empire is the loser's lot:
In liquid burnings, or on dry, to dwell,
Is all the sad variety of hell.
But see, the victor has recalled, from far,
The avenging storms, his ministers of war:
His shafts are spent, and his tired thunders sleep,
Nor longer bellow through the boundless deep.
Best take the occasion, and these waves forsake,
While time is given.—Ho, Asmoday, awake,
If thou art he! But ah! how changed from him,
Companion of my arms! how wan! how dim!
How faded all thy glories are! I see
Myself too well, and my own change in thee.

ASMODAY
Prince of the thrones, who in the fields of light
Led'st forth the embattled seraphim to fight;
Who shook the power of heaven's eternal state,
Had broke it too, if not upheld by fate;
But now those hopes are fled: Thus low we lie,
Shut from his day, and that contended sky,
And lost, as far as heavenly forms can die;
Yet, not all perished: We defy him still,
And yet wage war, with our unconquered will.

LUCIFER
Strength may return.

ASMODAY
Already of thy virtue I partake,
Erected by thy voice.

LUCIFER
See on the lake
Our troops, like scattered leaves in autumn, lie;

First let us raise ourselves, and seek the dry,
Perhaps more easy dwelling.

ASMODAY
From the beach
Thy well-known voice the sleeping gods will reach,
And wake the immortal sense, which thunder's noise
Had quelled, and lightning deep had driven within them.

LUCIFER
With wings expanded wide, ourselves we'll rear,
And fly incumbent on the dusky air.—
Hell, thy new lord receive!
Heaven cannot envy me an empire here.

[Both fly to dry Land.

ASMODAY
Thus far we have prevailed; if that be gain,
Which is but change of place, not change of pain.
Now summon we the rest.

LUCIFER
Dominions, Powers, ye chiefs of heaven's bright host,
(Of heaven, once your's; but now in battle lost)
Wake from your slumber! Are your beds of down?
Sleep you so easy there? Or fear the frown
Of him who threw you hence, and joys to see
Your abject state confess his victory?
Rise, rise, ere from his battlements he view
Your prostrate postures, and his bolts renew,
To strike you deeper down.

ASMODAY
They wake, they hear,
Shake off their slumber first, and next their fear;
And only for the appointed signal stay.

LUCIFER
Rise from the flood, and hither wing your way.

MOLOCH [From the Lake.]
Thine to command; our part is to obey.

[The rest of the **DEVILS** rise up, and fly to the Land.

LUCIFER
So, now we are ourselves again an host,

Fit to tempt fate, once more, for what we lost;
To o'erleap the etherial fence, or if so high
We cannot climb, to undermine his sky,
And blow him up, who justly rules us now,
Because more strong: Should he be forced to bow.
The right were ours again: 'Tis just to win
The highest place; to attempt, and fail, is sin.

MOLOCH
Changed as we are, we're yet from homage free;
We have, by hell, at least gained liberty:
That's worth our fall; thus low though we are driven,
Better to rule in hell, than serve in heaven.

LUCIFER
There spoke the better half of Lucifer!

ASMODAY
'Tis fit in frequent senate we confer,
And then determine how to steer our course;
To wage new war by fraud, or open force.
The doom's now past; submission were in vain.

MOLOCH
And were it not, such baseness I disdain;
I would not stoop, to purchase all above,
And should contemn a power, whom prayer could move,
As one unworthy to have conquered me.

BEELZEBUB
Moloch, in that all are resolved, like thee.
The means are unproposed; but 'tis not fit
Our dark divan in public view should sit;
Or what we plot against the Thunderer,
The ignoble crowd of vulgar devils hear.

LUCIFER
A golden palace let be raised on high;
To imitate? No, to outshine the sky!
All mines are ours, and gold above the rest:
Let this be done; and quick as 'twas exprest.

[A Palace rises, where sit, as in council, **LUCIFER, ASMODAY, MOLOCH, BELIAL, BEELZEBUB,** and **SATAN.**

Most high and mighty lords, who better fell
From heaven, to rise states-general of hell,
Nor yet repent, though ruined and undone,
Our upper provinces already won,

Such pride there is in souls created free,
Such hate of universal monarchy;
Speak, for we therefore meet:
If peace you chuse, your suffrages declare;
Or means propound, to carry on the war.

MOLOCH
My sentence is for war; that open too:
Unskilled in stratagems, plain force I know:
Treaties are vain to losers; nor would we,
Should heaven grant peace, submit to sovereignty.
We can no caution give we will adore;
And he above is warned to trust no more.
What then remains but battle?

SATAN
I agree
With this brave vote; and if in hell there be
Ten more such spirits, heaven is our own again:
We venture nothing, and may all obtain.
Yet who can hope but well, since even success
Makes foes secure, and makes our danger less?
Seraph and cherub, careless of their charge,
And wanton, in full ease now live at large;
Unguarded leave the passes of the sky,
And all dissolved in hallelujahs lie.

MOLOCH
Grant that our hazardous attempt prove vain;
We feel the worst, secured from greater pain:
Perhaps we may provoke the conquering foe
To make us nothing; yet, even then, we know,
That not to be, is not to be in woe.

BELIAL
That knowledge which, as spirits, we obtain,
Is to be valued in the midst of pain:
Annihilation were to lose heaven more;
We are not quite exiled where thought can soar.
Then cease from arms;
Tempt him not farther to pursue his blow,
And be content to bear those pains we know.
If what we had, we could not keep, much less
Can we regain what those above possess.

BEELZEBUB
Heaven sleeps not; from one wink a breach would be
In the full circle of eternity.

Long pains, with use of bearing, are half eased;
Heaven, unprovoked, at length may be appeased.
By war we cannot scape our wretched lot;
And may, perhaps, not warring, be forgot.

ASMODAY
Could we repent, or did not heaven well know
Rebellion, once forgiven, would greater grow,
I should, with Belial, chuse ignoble ease;
But neither will the conqueror give peace,
Nor yet so lost in this low state we are,
As to despair of a well-managed war.
Nor need we tempt those heights which angels keep,
Who fear no force, or ambush, from the deep.
What if we find some easier enterprise?
There is a place,—if ancient prophecies
And fame in heaven not err,—the blest abode
Of some new race, called Man, a demi-god,
Whom, near this time, the Almighty must create;
He swore it, shook the heavens, and made it fate.

LUCIFER
I heard it; through all heaven the rumour ran,
And much the talk of this intended Man:
Of form divine; but less in excellence
Than we; endued with reason lodged in sense:
The soul pure fire, like ours, of equal force;
But, pent in flesh, must issue by discourse:
We see what is; to Man truth must be brought
By sense, and drawn by a long chain of thought:
By that faint light, to will and understand;
For made less knowing, he's at more command.

ASMODAY
Though heaven be shut, that world, if it be made,
As nearest heaven, lies open to invade:
Man therefore must be known, his strength, his state,
And by what tenure he holds all of fate.
Him let us then seduce, or overthrow;
The first is easiest, and makes heaven his foe.
Advise, if this attempt be worth our care.

BELIAL
Great is the advantage, great the hazards are.
Some one (but who that task dares undertake?)
Of this new creature must discovery make.
Hell's brazen gates he first must break, then far
Must wander through old night, and through the war

Of antique chaos; and, when these are past,
Meet heaven's out-guards, who scout upon the waste:
At every station must be bid to stand,
And forced to answer every strict demand.

MOLOCH
This glorious enterprise—

[Rising up.

LUCIFER
Rash angel, stay;

[Rising, and laying his sceptre on **MOLOCH'S** head.

That palm is mine, which none shall take away.
Hot braves, like thee, may fight; but know not well
To manage this, the last great stake of hell.
Why am I ranked in state above the rest,
If, while I stand of sovereign power possest,
Another dares, in danger, farther go?
Kings are not made for ease, and pageant-show.
Who would be conqueror, must venture all:
He merits not to rise, who dares not fall.

ASMODAY
The praise, and danger, then, be all your own.

LUCIFER
On this foundation I erect my throne:
Through brazen gates, vast chaos, and old night,
I'll force my way, and upwards steer my flight;
Discover this new world, and newer Man;
Make him my footstep to mount heaven again:
Then, in the clemency of upward air,
We'll scour our spots, and the dire thunder scar,
With all the remnants of the unlucky war,
And once again grow bright, and once again grow fair.

ASMODAY
Meantime the youth of hell strict guard may keep,
And set their centries to the utmost deep,
That no etherial parasite may come
To spy our ills, and tell glad tales at home.

LUCIFER
Before yon brimstone lake thrice ebb and flow,
(Alas, that we must measure time by woe!)

I shall return, (my mind presages well)
And outward lead the colonies of hell.
Your care I much approve; what time remains,
Seek to forget, at least divert your pains
With sports and music, in the vales and fields,
And whate'erjoy so sad a climate yields.

[Betwixt the first Act and the second, while the Chiefs sit in the palace, may be expressed the sports of the Devils; as flights, and dancing in grotesque figures: And a song, expressing the change of their condition; what they enjoyed before, and how they fell bravely in battle, having deserved victory by their valour, and what they would have done if they had conquered.

ACT II

SCENE I—A Champaign Country

ADAM, as newly created, laid on a bed of moss and flowers, by a rock.

ADAM
What am I? or from whence? For that I am

[Rising.

I know, because I think; but whence I came,
Or how this frame of mine began to be,
What other being can disclose to me?
I move, I see, I speak, discourse, and know;
Though now I am, I was not always so.
Then that, from which I was, must be before,
Whom, as my spring of being, I adore.
How full of ornament is all I view,
In all its parts! and seems as beautiful as new:
O goodly-ordered work! O Power Divine,
Of thee I am, and what I am is thine!

[**RAPHAEL** descends to **ADAM**, in a cloud.

RAPHAEL
First of mankind, made o'er the world to reign,
Whose fruitful loins an unborn kind contain,
Well hast thou reasoned: Of himself is none
But that Eternal Infinite and One,
Who never did begin, who ne'er can end;
On Him all beings, as their source, depend.
We first, who of his image most partake,
Whom he all spirit, immortal, pure, did make;

Man next; whose race, exalted, must supply
The place of those, who, falling, lost the sky.

ADAM
Bright minister of heaven, sent here below
To me, who but begin to think and know;
If such could fall from bliss, who knew and saw,
By near admission, their creator's law,
What hopes have I, from heaven remote so far,
To keep those laws, unknowing when I err?

RAPHAEL
Right reason's law to every human heart
The Eternal, as his image, will impart:
This teaches to adore heaven's Majesty;
In prayer and praise does all devotion lie:
So doing, thou and all thy race are blest.

ADAM
Of every creeping thing, of bird, and beast,
I see the kinds: In pairs distinct they go;
The males their loves, their lovers females know:
Thou nam'st a race which must proceed from me,
Yet my whole species in myself I see:
A barren sex, and single, of no use,
But full of forms which I can ne'er produce.

RAPHAEL
Think not the Power, who made thee thus, can find
No way like theirs to propagate thy kind:
Meantime, live happy in thyself alone;
Like him who, single, fills the etherial throne.
To study nature will thy time employ:
Knowledge and innocence are perfect joy.

ADAM
If solitude were best, the All-wise above
Had made no creature for himself to love.
I add not to the power he had before;
Yet to make me, extends his goodness more.
He would not be alone, who all things can;
But peopled heaven with angels, earth with man.

RAPHAEL
As man and angels to the Deity,
So all inferior creatures are to thee.
Heaven's greatness no society can bear;
Servants he made, and those thou want'st not here.

ADAM
Why did he reason in my soul implant,
And speech, the effect of reason? To the mute,
My speech is lost; my reason to the brute.
Love and society more blessings bring
To them, the slaves, than power to me, their king.

RAPHAEL
Thus far to try thee; but to heaven 'twas known,
It was not best for man to be alone;
An equal, yet thy subject, is designed,
For thy soft hours, and to unbend thy mind.
Thy stronger soul shall her weak reason sway;
And thou, through love, her beauty shalt obey;
Thou shalt secure her helpless sex from harms,
And she thy cares shall sweeten with her charms.

ADAM
What more can heaven bestow, or man require?

RAPHAEL
Yes, he can give beyond thy own desire.
A mansion is provided thee, more fair
Than this, and worthy heaven's peculiar care:
Not framed of common earth, nor fruits, nor flowers
Of vulgar growth, but like celestial bowers:
The soil luxuriant, and the fruit divine,
Where golden apples on green branches shine,
And purple grapes dissolve into immortal wine;
For noon-day's heat are closer arbours made,
And for fresh evening air the opener glade.
Ascend; and, as we go,
More wonders thou shalt know.

ADAM
And, as we go, let earth and heaven above
Sound our great Maker's power, and greater love.

[They ascend to soft music, and a song is sung.

[The Scene changes, and represents, above, a Sun gloriously rising and moving orbicularly: at a distance, below, is the Moon; the part next the Sun enlightened, the other dark. A black Cloud comes whirling from the adverse part of the Heavens, bearing **LUCIFER** in it; at his nearer approach the body of the Sun is darkened.

LUCIFER
Am I become so monstrous, so disfigured,

That nature cannot suffer my approach,
Or look me in the face, but stands aghast;
And that fair light which gilds this new-made orb,
Shorn of his beams, shrinks in? accurst ambition!
And thou, black empire of the nether world,
How dearly have I bought you! But, 'tis past;
I have already gone too far to stop,
And must push on my dire revenge, in ruin
Of this gay frame, and man, my upstart rival,
In scorn of me created. Down, my pride,
And all my swelling thoughts! I must forget
Awhile I am a devil, and put on
A smooth submissive face; else I in vain
Have past through night and chaos, to discover
Those envied skies again, which I have lost.
But stay; far off I see a chariot driven,
Flaming with beams, and in it Uriel,
One of the seven, (I know his hated face)
Who stands in presence of the eternal throne,
And seems the regent of that glorious light.

[From that part of the Heavens where the Sun appears, a Chariot is discovered drawn with white Horses, and in it **URIEL**, the Regent of the Sun. The Chariot moves swiftly towards **LUCIFER**, and at **URIEL'S** approach the Sun recovers his light.

URIEL
Spirit, who art thou, and from whence arrived?
(For I remember not thy face in heaven)
Or by command, or hither led by choice?
Or wander'st thou within this lucid orb,
And, strayed from those fair fields of light above,
Amidst this new creation want'st a guide,
To reconduct thy steps?

LUCIFER
Bright Uriel,
Chief of the seven! thou flaming minister,
Who guard'st this new-created orb of light,
(The world's eye that, and thou the eye of it)
Thy favour and high office make thee known:
An humble cherub I, and of less note,
Yet bold, by thy permission, hither come,
On high discoveries bent.

URIEL
Speak thy design.

LUCIFER

Urged by renown of what I heard above,
Divulged by angels nearest heaven's high King,
Concerning this new world, I came to view
(If worthy such a favour) and admire
This last effect of our great Maker's power:
Thence to my wondering fellows I shall turn,
Full fraught with joyful tidings of these works,
New matter of his praise, and of our songs.

URIEL
Thy business is not what deserves my blame,
Nor thou thyself unwelcome; see, fair spirit,
Below yon sphere (of matter not unlike it)
There hangs the ball of earth and water mixt,
Self-centered and unmoved.

LUCIFER
But where dwells man?

URIEL
On yonder mount; thou see'st it fenced with rocks,
And round the ascent a theatre of trees,
A sylvan scene, which, rising by degrees,
Leads up the eye below, nor gluts the sight
With one full prospect, but invites by many,
To view at last the whole: There his abode,
Thither direct thy flight.

LUCIFER
O blest be thou,
Who to my low converse has lent thy ear,
And favoured my request! Hail, and farewell.

[Flies downward out of sight.

URIEL
Not unobserved thou goest, whoe'er thou art;
Whether some spirit on holy purpose bent,
Or some fallen angel from below broke loose,
Who com'st, with envious eyes and curst intent,
To view this world and its created lord:
Here will I watch, and, while my orb rolls on,
Pursue from hence thy much suspected flight,
And, if disguised, pierce through with beams of light.

[The Chariot drives forward out of sight.

SCENE II—Paradise

Trees cut out on each side, with several Fruits upon them; a Fountain in the midst: At the far end the prospect terminates in Walks.

ADAM
If this be dreaming, let me never wake;
But still the joys of that sweet sleep partake.
Methought—but why do I my bliss delay,
By thinking what I thought? Fair vision, stay;
My better half, thou softer part of me,
To whom I yield my boasted sovereignty,
I seek myself, and find not, wanting thee.

[Exit.

[Enter **EVE**.

EVE
Tell me, ye hills and dales, and thou fair sun,
Who shin'st above, what am I? Whence begun?
Like myself, I see nothing: From each tree
The feathered kind peep down to look on me;
And beasts with up-cast eyes forsake their shade,
And gaze, as if I were to be obeyed.
Sure I am somewhat which they wish to be,
And cannot; I myself am proud of me.
What's here? another firmament below,

[Looks into a fountain.

Spread wide, and other trees that downward grow!
And now a face peeps up, and now draws near,
With smiling looks, as pleased to see me here.
As I advance, so that advances too,
And seems to imitate whate'er I do:
When I begin to speak, the lips it moves;
Streams drown the voice, or it would say, it loves.
Yet when I would embrace, it will not stay:

[Stoops down to embrace.

Lost ere 'tis held; when nearest, far away.
Ah, fair, yet false! ah, Being, formed to cheat,
By seeming kindness, mixt with deep deceit!

[Enter **ADAM**.

ADAM
O virgin, heaven-begot, and born of man,
Thou fairest of thy great Creator's works!
Thee, goddess, thee the Eternal did ordain,
His softer substitute on earth to reign;
And, wheresoe'er thy happy footsteps tread,
Nature in triumph after thee is led!
Angels with pleasure view thy matchless grace,
And love their Maker's image in thy face.

EVE
O, only like myself,(for nothing here
So graceful, so majestic does appear:)
Art thou the form my longing eyes did see,
Loosed from thy fountain, and come out to me?
Yet sure thou art not, nor thy face the same,
Nor thy limbs moulded in so soft a frame;
Thou look'st more sternly, dost more strongly move,
And more of awe thou bear'st, and less of love.
Yet pleased I hear thee, and above the rest,
I, next myself, admire and love thee best.

ADAM
Made to command, thus freely I obey,
And at thy feet the whole creation lay.
Pity that love thy beauty does beget;
What more I shall desire, I know not yet.
First let us locked in close embraces be,
Thence I, perhaps, may teach myself and thee.

EVE
Somewhat forbids me, which I cannot name;
For, ignorant of guilt, I fear not shame:
But some restraining thought, I know not why,
Tells me, you long should beg, I long deny.

ADAM
In vain! my right to thee is sealed above;
Look round and see where thou canst place thy love:
All creatures else are much unworthy thee;
They matched, and thou alone art left for me.
If not to love, we both were made in vain;
I my new empire would resign again,
And change with my dumb slaves my nobler mind,
Who, void of reason, more of pleasure find.
Methinks, for me they beg; each silently
Demands thy grace, and seems to watch thy eye.

EVE
I well foresee, whene'er thy suit I grant,
That I my much-loved sovereignty shall want:
Or like myself some other may be made,
And her new beauty may thy heart invade.

ADAM
Could heaven some greater master-piece devise,
Set out with all the glories of the skies,
That beauty yet in vain he should decree.
Unless he made another heart for me.

EVE
With how much ease I, whom I love, believe!
Giving myself, my want of worth I grieve.
Here, my inviolable faith I plight,
So, thou be my defence, I, thy delight.

[Exeunt, he leading her.

ACT III

SCENE I—Paradise

LUCIFER.

LUCIFER
Fair place! yet what is this to heaven, where I
Sat next, so almost equalled the Most High?
I doubted, measuring both, who was more strong;
Then, willing to forget time since so long,
Scarce thought I was created: Vain desire
Of empire in my thoughts still shot me higher,
To mount above his sacred head: Ah why,
When he so kind, was so ungrateful I?
He bounteously bestowed unenvied good
On me: In arbitrary grace I stood:
To acknowledge this, was all he did exact;
Small tribute, where the will to pay was act.
I mourn it now, unable to repent,
As he, who knows my hatred to relent,
Jealous of power once questioned: Hope, farewell;
And with hope, fear; no depth below my hell
Can be prepared: Then, Ill, be thou my good;
And, vast destruction, be my envy's food.

Thus I, with heaven, divided empire gain;
Seducing man, I make his project vain,
And in one hour destroy his six days pain.
They come again, I must retire.

[Enter **ADAM** and **EVE**.

ADAM
Thus shall we live in perfect bliss, and see,
Deathless ourselves, our numerous progeny.
Thou young and beauteous, my desires to bless;
I, still desiring, what I still possess.

EVE
Heaven, from whence love, our greatest blessing, came,
Can give no more, but still to be the same.
Thou more of pleasure may'st with me partake;
I, more of pride, because thy bliss I make.

ADAM
When to my arms thou brought'st thy virgin love,
Fair angels sung our bridal hymn above:
The Eternal, nodding, shook the firmament,
And conscious nature gave her glad consent.
Roses unbid, and every fragrant flower,
Flew from their stalks, to strew thy nuptial bower:
The furred and feathered kind the triumph did pursue,
And fishes leaped above the streams, the passing pomp to view.

EVE
When your kind eyes looked languishing on mine,
And wreathing arms did soft embraces join,
A doubtful trembling seized me first all o'er;
Then, wishes; and a warmth, unknown before:
What followed was all ecstasy and trance;
Immortal pleasures round my swimming eyes did dance,
And speechless joys, in whose sweet tumult tost,
I thought my breath and my new being lost.

LUCIFER
O death to hear! and a worse hell on earth! [Aside.
What mad profusion on this clod-born birth!
Abyss of joys, as if heaven meant to shew
What, in base matters, such a hand could do:
Or was his virtue spent, and he no more
With angels could supply the exhausted store,
Of which I swept the sky?
And wanting subjects to his haughty will,

On this mean work employed his trifling skill?

EVE
Blest in ourselves, all pleasures else abound;
Without our care behold the unlaboured ground
Bounteous of fruit; above our shady bowers
The creeping jessamin thrusts her fragrant flowers;
The myrtle, orange, and the blushing rose,
With bending heaps so nigh their blooms disclose,
Each seems to swell the flavour which the other blows:
By these the peach, the guava, and the pine,
And, creeping 'twixt them all, the mantling vine
Does round their trunks her purple clusters twine.

ADAM
All these are ours, all nature's excellence,
Whose taste or smell can bless the feasted sense;
One only fruit, in the mid garden placed,—
The Tree of Knowledge,—is denied our taste;
(Our proof of duty to our Maker's will:)
Of disobedience, death's the threatened ill.

EVE
Death is some harm, which, though we know not yet,
Since threatened, we must needs imagine great:
And sure he merits it, who disobeys
That one command, and one of so much ease.

LUCIFER
Must they then die, if they attempt to know?
He sees they would rebel, and keeps them low.
On this foundation I their ruin lay,
Hope to know more shall tempt to disobey.
I fell by this, and, since their strength is less,
Why should not equal means give like success?

ADAM
Come, my fair love, our morning's task we lose;
Some labour even the easiest life would chuse:
Ours is not great: the dangling boughs to crop,
Whose too luxuriant growth our alleys stop,
And choke the paths: This our delight requires,
And heaven no more of daily work desires.

EVE
With thee to live, is paradise alone:
Without the pleasure of thy sight, is none.
I fear small progress will be made this day;

So much our kisses will our task delay.

[Exeunt.

LUCIFER
Why have not I, like these, a body too,
Formed for the same delights which they pursue!
I could (so variously my passions move)
Enjoy, and blast her in the act of love.
Unwillingly I hate such excellence;
She wronged me not; but I revenge the offence,
Through her, on heaven, whose thunder took away
My birth-right skies! Live happy whilst you may,
Blest pair; y'are not allowed another day!

[Exit.

GABRIEL and **ITHURIEL** descend, carried on bright clouds, and flying cross each other, then light on the ground.

GABRIEL
Ithuriel, since we two commissioned are
From heaven the guardians of this new made pair,
Each mind his charge; for, see, the night draws on,
And rising mists pursue the setting sun.

ITHURIEL
Blest is our lot to serve; our task we know:
To watch, lest any, from the abyss below
Broke loose, disturb their sleep with dreams; or worse,
Assault their beings with superior force.

[**URIEL** flies down from the Sun.

URIEL
Gabriel, if now the watch be set, prepare,
With strictest guard, to shew thy utmost care.
This morning came a spirit, fair he seemed,
Whom, by his face, I some young cherub deemed;
Of man he much inquired, and where his place,
With shews of zeal to praise his Maker's grace;
But I, with watchful eyes, observed his flight,
And saw him on yon steepy mount alight;
There, as he thought, unseen, he laid aside
His borrowed mask, and re-assumed his pride:
I marked his looks, averse to heaven and good;
Dusky he grew, and long revolving stood
On some deep, dark design; thence shot with haste,

And o'er the mounds of Paradise he past:
By his proud port, he seemed the Prince of Hell;
And here he lurks in shades 'till night: Search well
Each grove and thicket, pry in every shape,
Lest, hid in some, the arch hypocrite escape.

GABRIEL
If any spirit come to invade, or scout
From hell, what earthy fence can keep him out?
But rest secure of this, he shall be found,
And taken, or proscribed this happy ground.

ITHURIEL
Thou to the east, I westward walk the round,
And meet we in the midst.

URIEL
Heaven your design
Succeed; your charge requires you, and me mine.

[**URIEL** flies forward out of sight; the two **ANGELS** exeunt severally.

[A Night-piece of a pleasant Bower: **ADAM** and **EVE** asleep in it.

[Enter **LUCIFER**.

LUCIFER
So, now they lie secure in love, and steep
Their sated senses in full draughts of sleep.
By what sure means can I their bliss invade?
By violence? No, for they are immortal made.
Their reason sleeps, but mimic fancy wakes,
Supplies her part, and wild ideas takes,
From words and things, ill sorted and misjoined;
The anarchy of thought, and chaos of the mind:
Hence dreams, confused and various, may arise;
These will I set before the woman's eyes;
The weaker she, and made my easier prey;
Vain shows and pomp the softer sex betray.

[**LUCIFER** sits down by **EVE**, and seems to whisper in her ear.

[A Vision, where a tree rises loaden with fruit; **FOUR SPIRITS** rise with it, and draw a canopy out of the tree; other **SPIRITS** dance about the tree in deformed shapes; after the dance an **ANGEL** enters, with a **WOMAN**, habited like **EVE**.

ANGEL [Singing.]
Look up, look up, and see,

What heaven prepares for thee;
Look up, and this fair fruit behold,
Ruddy it smiles, and rich with streaks of gold.
The loaded branches downward bend,
Willing they stoop, and thy fair hand attend.
Fair mother of mankind, make haste
And bless, and bless thy senses with the taste.

WOMAN
No, 'tis forbidden; I
In tasting it shall die.

ANGEL
Say, who enjoined this harsh command?

WOMAN
'Twas heaven; and who can heaven withstand?

ANGEL
Why was it made so fair, why placed in sight?
Heaven is too good to envy man's delight.
See, we before thy face will try
What thou so fearest, and will not die.

[The **ANGEL** takes the fruit, and gives to the **SPIRITS** who danced; they immediately put off their deformed shapes, and appear **ANGELS**.

ANGEL [Singing.]
Behold what a change on a sudden is here!
How glorious in beauty, how bright they appear!
Prom spirits deformed they are deities made,
Their pinions at pleasure the clouds can invade,

[The **ANGEL** gives to the **WOMAN**, who eats.

Till equal in honour they rise,
With him who commands in the skies;
Then taste without fear, and be happy and wise.

WOMAN
Ah, now I believe! such a pleasure I find,
As enlightens my eyes, and enlivens my mind.

[The **SPIRITS**, who are turned **ANGELS**, fly up when they have tasted.

I only repent,
I deferred my content.

ANGEL
Now wiser experience has taught you to prove,
What a folly it is,
Out of fear to shun bliss.
To the joy that's forbidden we eagerly move;
It inhances the price, and increases the love.

CHORUS OF BOTH
To the joy, &c.

[Two **ANGELS** descend; they take the **WOMAN** each by the hand, and fly up with her out of sight. The **ANGEL** who sung, and the **SPIRITS** who held the canopy, at the same instant sink down with the tree.

[Enter **GABRIEL** and **ITHURIEL** to **LUCIFER**, who remains.

GABRIEL
What art thou? speak thy name and thy intent.
Why here alone? and on what errand sent?
Not from above; no, thy wan looks betray
Diminished light, and eyes unused to day.

LUCIFER
Not to know me, argues thyself unknown:
Time was, when, shining next the imperial throne,
I sat in awful state; while such as thou
Did in the ignoble crowd at distance bow.

GABRIEL
Think'st thou, vain spirit, thy glories are the same?
And seest not sin obscures thy god-like frame?
I know thee now by thy ungrateful pride,
That shews me what thy faded looks did hide,
Traitor to Him who made and set thee high,
And fool, that Power which formed thee to defy.

LUCIFER
Go, slaves, return, and fawn in heaven again:
Seek thanks from him whose quarrel you maintain.
Vile wretches! of your servitude to boast;
You basely keep the place I bravely lost.

ITHURIEL
Freedom is choice of what we will and do:
Then blame not servants, who are freely so.
'Tis base not to acknowledge what we owe.

LUCIFER
Thanks, howe'er due, proclaim subjection yet;

I fought for power to quit the upbraided debt.
Whoe'er expects our thanks, himself repays,
And seems but little, who can want our praise.

GABRIEL
What in us duty, shews not want in him;
Blest in himself alone,
To whom no praise we, by good deeds, can add;
Nor can his glory suffer from our bad.
Made for his use; yet he has formed us so,
We, unconstrained, what he commands us do.
So praise we him, and serve him freely best;
Thus thou, by choice, art fallen, and we are blest.

ITHURIEL
This, lest thou think thy plea, unanswered, good.
Our question thou evad'st: How didst thou dare
To break hell bounds, and near this human pair
In nightly ambush lie?

LUCIFER
Lives there, who would not seek to force his way,
From pain to ease, from darkness to the day?
Should I, who found the means to 'scape, not dare
To change my sulphurous smoke for upper air?
When I, in fight, sustained your Thunderer,
And heaven on me alone spent half his war,
Think'st thou those wounds were light? Should I not seek
The clemency of some more temperate clime,
To purge my gloom; and, by the sun refined,
Bask in his beams, and bleach me in the wind?

GABRIEL
If pain to shun be all thy business here,
Methinks thy fellows the same course should steer.
Is their pain less, who yet behind thee stay?
Or thou less hardy to endure than they?

LUCIFER
Nor one, nor t'other; but, as leaders ought,
I ventured first alone, first danger sought,
And first explored this new-created frame,
Which filled our dusky regions with its fame;
In hopes my fainting troops to settle here,
And to defend against your Thunderer,
This spot of earth; or nearer heaven repair,
And forage to his gates from middle air.

ITHURIEL
Fool! to believe thou any part canst gain
From Him, who could'st not thy first ground maintain.

GABRIEL
But whether that design, or one as vain,
To attempt the lives of these, first drew thee here,
Avoid the place, and never more appear
Upon this hallowed earth; else prove our might.

LUCIFER
Not that I fear, do I decline the fight:
You I disdain; let me with Him contend,
On whom your limitary powers depend.
More honour from the sender than the sent:
Till then, I have accomplished my intent;
And leave this place, which but augments my pain,
Gazing to wish, yet hopeless to obtain.

[Exit, they following him.

ACT IV

SCENE I—Paradise

ADAM and **EVE**.

ADAM
Strange was your dream, and full of sad portent;
Avert it, heaven, if it from heaven were sent!
Let on thy foes the dire presages fall;
To us be good and easy, when we call.

EVE
Behold from far a breaking cloud appears,
Which in it many winged warriors bears:
Their glory shoots upon my aching sense;
Thou, stronger, mayest endure the flood of light,
And while in shades I chear my fainting sight,
Encounter the descending Excellence.

[Exit.

[The Cloud descends with **SIX ANGELS** in it, and when it is near the ground, breaks, and on each side discovers six more: They descend out of the Cloud. **RAPHAEL** and **GABRIEL** discourse with **ADAM**, the rest stand at a distance.

RAPHAEL
First of mankind, that we from heaven are sent,
Is from heaven's care thy ruin to prevent.
The Apostate Angel has by night been here,
And whispered through thy sleeping consort's ear
Delusive dreams. Thus warned by us, beware,
And guide her frailty by thy timely care.

GABRIEL
These, as thy guards from outward harms, are sent;
Ills from within thy reason must prevent.

ADAM
Natives of heaven, who in compassion deign
To want that place where joys immortal reign,
In care of me; what praises can I pay,
Descended in obedience; taught to obey?

RAPHAEL
Praise Him alone, who god-like formed thee free,
With will unbounded as a deity;
Who gave thee reason, as thy aid, to chuse
Apparent good, and evil to refuse.
Obedience is that good; this heaven exacts,
And heaven, all-just, from man requires not acts,
Which man wants power to do: Power then is given
Of doing good, but not compelled by heaven.

GABRIEL
Made good, that thou dost to thy Maker owe;
But to thyself, if thou continuest so.

ADAM
Freedom of will of all good things is best;
But can it be by finite man possest?
I know not how heaven can communicate
What equals man to his Creator's state.

RAPHAEL
Heaven cannot give his boundless power away,
But boundless liberty of choice he may;
So orbs from the first Mover motion take,
Yet each their proper revolutions make.

ADAM
Grant heaven could once have given us liberty;
Are we not bounded now, by firm decree,

Since whatsoe'er is pre-ordained must be?
Else heaven for man events might pre-ordain,
And man's free will might make those orders vain.

GABRIEL
The Eternal, when he did the world create,
All other agents did necessitate:
So what he ordered, they by nature do;
Thus light things mount, and heavy downward go.
Man only boasts an arbitrary state.

ADAM
Yet causes their effects necessitate
In willing agents: Where is freedom then?
Or who can break the chain which limits men
To act what is unchangeably forecast,
Since the first cause gives motion to the last?

RAPHAEL
Heaven, by fore-knowing what will surely be,
Does only, first, effects in causes see,
And finds, but does not make, necessity.
Creation is of power and will the effect,
Foreknowledge only of his intellect.
His prescience makes not, but supposes things;
Infers necessity to be, not brings.
Thus thou art not constrained to good or ill;
Causes, which work the effect, force not the will.

ADAM
The force unseen, and distant, I confess;
But the long chain makes not the bondage less.
Even man himself may to himself seem free;
And think that choice, which is necessity.

GABRIEL
And who but man should judge of man's free state?

ADAM
I find that I can chuse to love or hate,
Obey or disobey, do good or ill;
Yet such a choice is but consent, not will.
I can but chuse what he at first designed,
For he, before that choice, my will confined.

GABRIEL
Such impious fancies, where they entrance gain,
Make heaven, all-pure, thy crimes to pre-ordain.

ADAM
Far, far from me be banished such a thought,
I argue only to be better taught.
Can there be freedom, when what now seems free
Was founded on some first necessity?
For whate'er cause can move the will t'elect,
Must be sufficient to produce the effect;
And what's sufficient must effectual be:
Then how is man, thus forced by causes, free?

RAPHAEL
Sufficient causes only work the effect,
When necessary agents they respect.
Such is not man; who, though the cause suffice,
Yet often he his free assent denies.

ADAM
What causes not, is not sufficient still.

GABRIEL
Sufficient in itself; not in thy will.

RAPHAEL
When we see causes joined to effects at last,
The chain but shews necessity that's past.
That what's done is: (ridiculous proof of fate!)
Tell me which part it does necessitate?
I'll cruise the other; there I'll link the effect.
O chain, which fools, to catch themselves, project!

ADAM
Though no constraint from heaven, or causes, be,
Heaven may prevent that ill he does foresee;
And, not preventing, though he does not cause,
He seems to will that men should break his laws.

GABRIEL
Heaven may permit, but not to ill consent;
For, hindering ill, he would all choice prevent.
'Twere to unmake, to take away the will.

ADAM
Better constrained to good, than free to ill.

RAPHAEL
But what reward or punishment could be,
If man to neither good nor ill were free?

The eternal justice could decree no pain
To him whose sins itself did first ordain;
And good, compelled, could no reward exact:
His power would shine in goodness, not thy act.
Our task is done: Obey; and, in that choice,
Thou shalt be blest, and angels shall rejoice.

[**RAPHAEL** and **GABRIEL** fly up in the Cloud: the other **ANGELS** go off.

ADAM
Hard state of life! since heaven foreknows my will,
Why am I not tied up from doing ill?
Why am I trusted with myself at large,
When he's more able to sustain the charge?
Since angels fell, whose strength was more than mine,
'Twould show more grace my frailty to confine.
Fore-knowing the success, to leave me free,
Excuses him, and yet supports not me.

[To him **EVE**.

EVE
Behold, my heart's dear lord, how high the sun
Is mounted, yet our labour not begun.
The ground, unhid, gives more than we can ask;
But work is pleasure when we chuse our task.
Nature, not bounteous now, but lavish grows;
Our paths with flowers she prodigally strows;
With pain we lift up our entangled feet,
While cross our walks the shooting branches meet.

ADAM
Well has thy care advised; 'tis fit we haste;
Nature's too kind, and follows us too fast;
Leaves us no room her treasures to possess,
But mocks our industry with her excess;
And, wildly wanton, wears by night away
The sign of all our labours done by day.

EVE
Since, then, the work's so great, the hands so few,
This day let each a several task pursue.
By thee, my hands to labour will not move,
But, round thy neck, employ themselves in love.
When thou would'st work, one tender touch, one smile
(How can I hold?) will all thy task beguile.

ADAM

So hard we are not to our labour tied,
That smiles, and soft endearments are denied;
Smiles, not allowed to beasts, from reason move,
And are the privilege of human love:
And if, sometimes, each others eyes we meet,
Those little vacancies from toil are sweet.
But you, by absence, would refresh your joys,
Because perhaps my conversation cloys.
Yet this, would prudence grant, I could permit.

EVE
What reason makes my small request unfit?

ADAM
The fallen archangel, envious of our state,
Pursues our beings with immortal hate;
And, hopeless to prevail by open force,
Seeks hid advantage to betray us worse;
Which when asunder will not prove so hard;
For both together are each other's guard.

EVE
Since he, by force, is hopeless to prevail,
He can by fraud alone our minds assail:
And to believe his wiles my truth can move,
Is to misdoubt my reason, or my love.

ADAM
Call it my care, and not mistrust of thee;
Yet thou art weak, and full of art is he;
Else how could he that host seduce to sin,
Whose fall has left the heavenly nation thin?

EVE
I grant him armed with subtilty and hate;
But why should we suspect our happy state?
Is our perfection of so frail a make,
As every plot can undermine or shake?
Think better both of heaven, thyself, and me:
Who always fears, at ease can never be.
Poor state of bliss, where so much care is shown,
As not to dare to trust ourselves alone!

ADAM
Such is our state, as not exempt from fall;
Yet firm, if reason to our aid we call:
And that, in both, is stronger than in one;
I would not,—why would'st thou, then, be alone?

EVE
Because, thus warned, I know myself secure,
And long my little trial to endure,
To approve my faith, thy needless fears remove,
Gain thy esteem, and so deserve thy love.
If all this shake not thy obdurate will,
Know that, even present, I am absent still:
And then what pleasure hop'st thou in my stay,
When I'm constrained, and wish myself away?

ADAM
Constraint does ill with love and beauty suit;
I would persuade, but not be absolute.
Better be much remiss, than too severe;
If pleased in absence thou wilt still be here.
Go; in thy native innocence proceed,
And summon all thy reason at thy need.

EVE
My soul, my eyes delight! in this I find
Thou lov'st; because to love is to be kind.

[Embracing him.

Seeking my trial, I am still on guard:
Trials, less sought, would find us less prepared.
Our foe's too proud the weaker to assail,
Or doubles his dishonour if he fail.

[Exit.

ADAM
In love, what use of prudence can there be?
More perfect I, and yet more powerful she.
Blame me not, heaven; if thou love's power hast tried,
What could be so unjust to be denied?
One look of hers my resolution breaks;
Reason itself turns folly when she speaks:
And awed by her, whom it was made to sway,
Flatters her power, and does its own betray.

[Exit.

[The middle part of the Garden is represented, where four Rivers meet: On the right side of the Scene is placed the Tree of Life; on the left, the Tree of Knowledge.

[Enter **LUCIFER**.

LUCIFER
Methinks the beauties of this place should mourn;
The immortal fruits and flowers, at my return,
Should hang their withered heads; for sure my breath
Is now more poisonous, and has gathered death
Enough, to blast the whole creation's frame.
Swoln with despite, with sorrow, and with shame,
Thrice have I beat the wing, and rode with night
About the world, behind the globe of light,
To shun the watch of heaven; such care I use:
(What pains will malice, raised like mine, refuse?
Not the most abject form of brutes to take.)
Hid in the spiry volumes of the snake,
I lurked within the covert of a brake,
Not yet descried. But see, the woman here
Alone! beyond my hopes! no guardian near.
Good omen that: I must retire unseen,
And, with my borrowed shape, the work begin.

[Retires.

[Enter **EVE**.

EVE
Thus far, at least, with leave; nor can it be
A sin to look on this celestial tree:
I would not more; to touch, a crime may prove:
Touching is a remoter taste in love.
Death may be there, or poison in the smell,
(If death in any thing so fair can dwell:)
But heaven forbids: I could be satisfied,
Were every tree but this, but this denied.

[A **SERPENT** enters on the Stage, and makes directly to the Tree of Knowledge, on which winding himself, he plucks an Apple; then descends, and carries it away.

Strange sight! did then our great Creator grant
That privilege, which we, their masters, want,
To these inferior brings? Or was it chance?
And was he blest with bolder ignorance?
I saw his curling crest the trunk enfold:
The ruddy fruit, distinguished o'er with gold.
And smiling in its native wealth, was torn
From the rich bough, and then in triumph borne:
The venturous victor marched unpunished hence,
And seemed to boast his fortunate offence.

[To her **LUCIFER**, in a human Shape.

LUCIFER
Hail, sovereign of this orb! formed to possess
The world, and, with one look, all nature bless.
Nature is thine; thou, empress, dost bestow
On fruits, to blossom; and on flowers, to blow.
They happy, yet insensible to boast
Their bliss: More happy they who know thee most.
Then happiest I, to human reason raised,
And voice, with whose first accents thou art praised.

EVE
What art thou, or from whence? For on this ground,
Beside my lord's, ne'er heard I human sound.
Art thou some other Adam, formed from earth,
And comest to claim an equal share, by birth,
In this fair field? Or sprung of heavenly race?

LUCIFER
An humble native of this happy place,
Thy vassal born, and late of lowest kind,
Whom heaven neglecting made, and scarce designed,
But threw me in, for number, to the rest,
Below the mounting bird and grazing beast;
By chance, not prudence, now superior grown.

EVE
To make thee such, what miracle was shown?

LUCIFER
Who would not tell what thou vouchsaf'st to hear?
Sawest thou not late a speckled serpent rear
His gilded spires to climb on yon' fair tree?
Before this happy minute I was he.

EVE
Thou speak'st of wonders: Make thy story plain.

LUCIFER
Not wishing then, and thoughtless to obtain
So great a bliss, but led by sense of good,
Inborn to all, I sought my needful food:
Then, on that heavenly tree my sight I cast;
The colour urged my eye, the scent my taste.
Not to detain thee long,—I took, did eat:
Scarce had my palate touched the immortal meat,
But, on a sudden, turned to what I am,

God-like, and, next to thee, I fair became;
Thought, spake, and reasoned; and, by reason found
Thee, nature's queen, with all her graces crowned.

EVE
Happy thy lot; but far unlike is mine:
Forbid to eat, not daring to repine.
'Twas heaven's command; and should we disobey,
What raised thy being, ours must take away.

LUCIFER
Sure you mistake the precept, or the tree:
Heaven cannot envious of his blessings be.
Some chance-born plant he might forbid your use,
As wild, or guilty of a deadly juice;
Not this, whose colour, scent divine, and taste,
Proclaim the thoughtful Maker not in haste.

EVE
By all these signs, too well I know the fruit,
And dread a Power severe and absolute.

LUCIFER
Severe, indeed; even to injustice hard;
If death, for knowing more, be your reward:
Knowledge of good, is good, and therefore fit;
And to know ill, is good, for shunning it.

EVE
What, but our good, could he design in this,
Who gave us all, and placed in perfect bliss?

LUCIFER
Excuse my zeal, fair sovereign, in your cause,
Which dares to tax his arbitrary laws.
'Tis all his aim to keep you blindly low,
That servile fear from ignorance may flow:
We scorn to worship whom too well we know.
He knows, that, eating, you shall godlike be;
As wise, as fit to be adored, as he.
For his own interest he this law has given;
Such beauty may raise factions in his heaven.
By awing you he does possession keep,
And is too wise to hazard partnership.

EVE
Alas, who dares dispute with him that right?
The Power, which formed us, must be infinite.

LUCIFER
Who told you how your form was first designed?
The sun and earth produce, of every kind,
Grass, flowers, and fruits; nay, living creatures too:
Their mould was base; 'twas more refined in you:
Where vital heat, in purer organs wrought,
Produced a nobler kind raised up to thought;
And that, perhaps, might his beginning be:
Something was first; I question if 'twere he.
But grant him first, yet still suppose him good,
Not envying those he made, immortal food.

EVE
But death our disobedience must pursue.

LUCIFER
Behold, in me, what shall arrive to you.
I tasted; yet I live: Nay, more; have got
A state more perfect than my native lot.
Nor fear this petty fault his wrath should raise:
Heaven rather will your dauntless virtue praise,
That sought, through threatened death, immortal good:
Gods are immortal only by their food.
Taste, and remove
What difference does 'twixt them and you remain;
As I gained reason, you shall godhead gain.

EVE
He eats, and lives, in knowledge greater grown: [Aside.
Was death invented then for us alone?
Is intellectual food to man denied,
Which brutes have with so much advantage tried?
Nor only tried themselves, but frankly, more,
To me have offered their unenvied store?

LUCIFER
Behold, and all your needless doubts remove;
View well this tree, (the queen of all the grove)
How vast her hole, how wide her arms are spread,
How high above the rest she shoots her head,
Placed in the midst: would heaven his work disgrace,
By planting poison in the happiest place?

Haste; you lose time and godhead by delay.

[Plucking the fruit.

EVE
'Tis done; I'll venture all, and disobey.

[Looking about her.
Perhaps, far hid in heaven, he does not spy,
And none of all his hymning guards are nigh.
To my dear lord the lovely fruit I'll bear;
He, to partake my bliss, my crime shall share.

[Exit hastily.

LUCIFER
She flew, and thanked me not, for haste: 'Twas hard,
With no return such counsel to reward.
My work is done, or much the greater part;
She's now the tempter to ensnare his heart.
He, whose firm faith no reason could remove,
Will melt before that soft seducer, love.

[Exit.

ACT V

SCENE I—Paradise

EVE, with a bough in her hand.

EVE
Methinks I tread more lightly on the ground;
My nimble feet from unhurt flowers rebound:
I walk in air, and scorn this earthly seat;
Heaven is my palace; this my base retreat.
Take me not, heaven, too soon; 'twill be unkind
To leave the partner of my bed behind.
I love the wretch; but stay, shall I afford
Him part? already he's too much my lord.
'Tis in my power to be a sovereign now;
And, knowing more, to make his manhood bow.
Empire is sweet; but how if heaven has spied?
If I should die, and He above provide
Some other Eve, and place her in my stead?
Shall she possess his love, when I am dead?
No; he shall eat, and die with me, or live:
Our equal crimes shall equal fortune give.

[Enter **ADAM**.

ADAM
What joy, without your sight, has earth, in store!
While you were absent, Eden was no more.
Winds murmured through the leaves your long delay,
And fountains, o'er the pebbles, chid your stay:
But with your presence cheered, they cease to mourn,
And walks wear fresher green at your return.

EVE
Henceforth you never shall have cause to chide;
No future absence shall our joys divide:
'Twas a short death my love ne'er tried before,
And therefore strange; but yet the cause was more.

ADAM
My trembling heart forebodes some ill; I fear
To ask that cause which I desire to hear.
What means that lovely fruit? what means, alas!
That blood, which flushes guilty in your face?
Speak—do not—yet, at last, I must be told.

EVE
Have courage, then: 'tis manly to be bold.
This fruit—why dost thou shake? no death is nigh:
'Tis what I tasted first; yet do not die.

ADAM
Is it—(I dare not ask it all at first;
Doubt is some ease to those who fear the worst:)
Say, 'tis not—

EVE
'Tis not what thou needst to fear:
What danger does in this fair fruit appear?
We have been cozened; and had still been so,
Had I not ventured boldly first to know.
Yet, not I first; I almost blush to say,
The serpent eating taught me first the way.
The serpent tasted, and the godlike fruit
Gave the dumb voice; gave reason to the brute.

ADAM
O fairest of all creatures, last and best
Of what heaven made, how art them dispossest
Of all thy native glories! fallen! decayed!
(Pity so rare a frame so frail was made)
Now cause of thy own ruin; and with thine,

(Ah, who can live without thee!) cause of mine.

EVE
Reserve thy pity till I want it more:
I know myself much happier than before;
More wise, more perfect, all I wish to be,
Were I but sure, alas! of pleasing thee.

ADAM
You've shown, how much you my content design:
Yet, ah! would heaven's displeasure pass like mine!
Must I without you, then, in wild woods dwell?
Think, and but think, of what I loved so well?
Condemned to live with subjects ever mute;
A savage prince, unpleased, though absolute?

EVE
Please then yourself with me, and freely taste,
Lest I, without you, should to godhead haste:
Lest, differing in degree, you claim too late
Unequal love, when 'tis denied by fate.

ADAM
Cheat not yourself with dreams of deity;
Too well, but yet too late, your crime I see:
Nor think the fruit your knowledge does improve;
But you have beauty still, and I have love.
Not cozened, I with choice my life resign:
Imprudence was your fault, but love was mine.

[Takes the fruit and eats it.

EVE
O wondrous power of matchless love exprest!

[Embracing him.

Why was this trial thine, of loving best?
I envy thee that lot; and could it be,
Would venture something more than death for thee.
Not that I fear, that death the event can prove;
Ware both immortal, while so well we love.

ADAM
Whate'er shall be the event, the lot is cast;
Where appetites are given, what sin to taste?
Or if a sin, 'tis but by precept such;
The offence so small, the punishment's too much.

To seek so soon his new-made world's decay:
Nor we, nor that, were fashioned for a day.

EVE
Give to the winds thy fear of death, or ill;
And think us made but for each other's will.

ADAM
I will, at least, defer that anxious thought,
And death, by fear, shall not be nigher brought:
If he will come, let us to joys make haste;
Then let him seize us when our pleasure's past.
We'll take up all before; and death shall find
We have drained life, and left a void behind.

[Exeunt.

[Enter **LUCIFER**.

LUCIFER
'Tis done:
Sick Nature, at that instant, trembled round;
And mother Earth sighed, as she felt the wound.
Of how short durance was this new-made state!
How far more mighty than heaven's love, hell's hate!
His project ruined, and his king of clay:
He formed an empire for his foe to sway.
Heaven let him rule, which by his arms he got;
I'm pleased to have obtained the second lot.
This earth is mine; whose lord I made my thrall:
Annexing to my crown his conquered ball.
Loosed from the lakes my regions I will lead,
And o'er the darkened air black banners spread:
Contagious damps, from hence, shall mount above,
And force him to his inmost heaven's remove.

[A clap of thunder is heard.

He hears already, and I boast too soon;
I dread that engine which secured his throne.
I'll dive below his wrath, into the deep,
And waste that empire, which I cannot keep.

[Sinks down.

[**RAPHAEL** and **GABRIEL** descend.

RAPHAEL

As much of grief as happiness admits
In heaven, on each celestial forehead sits:
Kindness for man, and pity for his fate,
May mix with bliss, and yet not violate.
Their heavenly harps a lower strain began;
And, in soft music, mourned the fall of man.

GABRIEL
I saw the angelic guards from earth ascend,
(Grieved they must now no longer man attend:)
The beams about their temples dimly shone;
One would have thought the crime had been their own.
The etherial people flocked for news in haste,
Whom they, with down-cast looks, and scarce saluting past:
While each did, in his pensive breast, prepare
A sad account of their successless care.

RAPHAEL
The Eternal yet, in majesty severe,
And strictest justice, did mild pity bear:
Their deaths deferred; and banishment, (their doom,)
In penitence foreseen, leaves mercy room.

GABRIEL
That message is thy charge: Mine leads me hence;
Placed at the garden's gate, for its defence,
Lest man, returning, the blest place pollute,
And 'scape from death, by life's immortal fruit.

[Another clap of thunder. Exeunt severally.

[Enter **ADAM** and **EVE,** affrighted.

ADAM
In what dark cavern shall I hide my head?
Where seek retreat, now innocence is fled?
Safe in that guard, I durst even hell defy;
Without it, tremble now, when heaven is nigh.

EVE
What shall we do? or where direct our flight?
Eastward, as far as I could cast my sight,
From opening heavens, I saw descending light.
Its glittering through the trees I still behold;
The cedar tops seem all to burn with gold.

ADAM
Some shape divine, whose beams I cannot bear!

Would I were hid, where light could not appear.
Deep into some thick covert would I run,
Impenetrable to the stars or sun,
And fenced from day, by night's eternal skreen;
Unknown to heaven, and to myself unseen.

EVE
In vain: What hope to shun his piercing sight,
Who from dark chaos struck the sparks of light?

ADAM
These should have been your thoughts, when, parting hence,
You trusted to your guideless innocence.
See now the effects of your own wilful mind:
Guilt walks before us; death pursues behind.
So fatal 'twas to seek temptations out:
Most confidence has still most cause to doubt.

EVE
Such might have been thy hap, alone assailed;
And so, together, might we both have failed.
Cursed vassalage of all my future kind!
First idolized, till love's hot fire be o'er,
Then slaves to those who courted us before.

ADAM
I counselled you to stay; your pride refused:
By your own lawless will you stand accused.

EVE
Have you that privilege of only wise,
And would you yield to her you so despise?
You should have shown the authority you boast,
And, sovereign-like, my headlong will have crost:
Counsel was not enough to sway my heart;
An absolute restraint had been your part.

ADAM
Even such returns do they deserve to find,
When force is lawful, who are fondly kind.
Unlike my love; for when thy guilt I knew,
I shared the curse which did that crime pursue.
Hard fate of love! which rigour did forbear,
And now 'tis taxed, because 'twas not severe.

EVE
You have yourself your kindness overpaid;
He ceases to oblige, who can upbraid.

ADAM
On women's virtue, who too much rely,
To boundless will give boundless liberty.
Restraint you will not brook; but think it hard
Your prudence is not trusted as your guard:
And, to yourselves so left, if ill ensues,
You first our weak indulgence will accuse.
Curst be that hour,
When, sated with my single happiness,
I chose a partner, to controul my bliss!
Who wants that reason which her will should sway,
And knows but just enough to disobey.

EVE
Better with brutes my humble lot had gone;
Of reason void, accountable for none:
The unhappiest of creation is a wife,
Made lowest, in the highest rank of life:
Her fellow's slave; to know, and not to chuse:
Curst with that reason she must never use.

ADAM
Add, that she's proud, fantastic, apt to change,
Restless at home, and ever prone to range:
With shows delighted, and so vain is she,
She'll meet the devil, rather than not see.
Our wise Creator, for his choirs divine,
Peopled his heaven with souls all masculine.—
Ah! why must man from woman take his birth?
Why was this sin of nature made on earth?
This fair defect, this helpless aid, called wife;
The bending crutch of a decrepid life?
Posterity no pairs from you shall find,
But such as by mistake of love are joined:
The worthiest men their wishes ne'er shall gain;
But see the slaves they scorn their loves obtain.
Blind appetite shall your wild fancies rule;
False to desert, and faithful to a fool.

[Turns in anger from her, and is going off.

EVE
Unkind! wilt thou forsake me, in distress,

[Kneeling.

For that which now is past me to redress?

I have misdone, and I endure the smart,
Loth to acknowledge, but more loth to part.
The blame be mine; you warned, and I refused:
What would you more? I have myself accused.
Was plighted faith so weakly sealed above,
That, for one error, I must lose your love?
Had you so erred, I should have been more kind,
Than to add pain to an afflicted mind.

ADAM
You're grown much humbler than you were before;
I pardon you; but see my face no more.

EVE
Vain pardon, which includes a greater ill;
Be still displeased, but let me see you still.
Without your much-loved sight I cannot live;
You more than kill me, if you so forgive.
The beasts, since we are fallen, their lords despise;
And, passing, look at me with glaring eyes:
Must I then wander helpless, and alone?
You'll pity me, too late, when I am gone.

ADAM
Your penitence does my compassion move;
As you deserve it, I may give my love.

EVE
On me, alone, let heaven's displeasure fall;
You merit none, and I deserve it all.

ADAM
You all heaven's wrath! how could you bear a part,
Who bore not mine, but with a bleeding heart?
I was too stubborn, thus to make you sue;
Forgive me—I am more in fault than you.
Return to me, and to my love return;
And, both offending, for each other mourn.

[Enter **RAPHAEL**.

RAPHAEL
Of sin to warn thee I before was sent;
For sin, I now pronounce thy punishment:
Yet that much lighter than thy crimes require;
Th' All-good does not his creatures' death desire:
Justice must punish the rebellious deed;
Yet punish so, as pity shall exceed.

ADAM
I neither can dispute his will, nor dare:
Death will dismiss me from my future care,
And lay me softly in my native dust,
To pay the forfeit of ill-managed trust.

EVE
Why seek you death? consider, ere you speak,
The laws were hard, the power to keep them, weak.
Did we solicit heaven to mould our clay?
From darkness to produce us to the day?
Did we concur to life, or chuse to be?
Was it our will which formed, or was it He?
Since 'twas his choice, not ours, which placed us here,
The laws we did not chuse why should we bear?

ADAM
Seek not, in vain, our Maker to accuse;
Terms were proposed; power left us to refuse.
The good we have enjoyed from heaven's free will,
And shall we murmur to endure the ill?
Should we a rebel son's excuse receive,
Because he was begot without his leave?
Heaven's right in us is more: first, formed to serve;
The good, we merit not; the ill, deserve.

RAPHAEL
Death is deferred, and penitence has room
To mitigate, if not reverse the doom:
But, for your crime, the Eternal does ordain
In Eden you no longer shall remain.
Hence, to the lower world, you are exiled;
This place with crimes shall be no more defiled.

EVE
Must we this blissful paradise forego?

RAPHAEL
Your lot must be where thorns and thistles grow,
Unhid, as balm and spices did at first;
For man, the earth, of which he was, is cursed.
By thy own toil procured, thou food shalt eat;   [To **ADAM**.
And know no plenty, but from painful sweat.
She, by a curse, of future wives abhorred,
Shall pay obedience to her lawful lord;
And he shall rule, and she in thraldom live,
Desiring more of love than man can give.

ADAM
Heaven is all mercy; labour I would chuse;
And could sustain this paradise to lose:
The bliss, but not the place: Here, could I say,
Heaven's winged messenger did pass the day;
Under this pine the glorious angel staid:
Then, show my wondering progeny the shade.
In woods and lawns, where-e'er thou didst appear,
Each place some monument of thee should bear.
I, with green turfs, would grateful altars raise,
And heaven, with gums, and offered incense, praise.

RAPHAEL
Where-e'er thou art, He is; the Eternal Mind
Acts through all places; is to none confined:
Fills ocean, earth, and air, and all above,
And through the universal mass does move.
Thou canst be no where distant: Yet this place
Had been thy kingly seat, and here thy race,
From all the ends of peopled earth had come
To reverence thee, and see their native home.
Immortal, then; now sickness, care, and age,
And war, and luxury's more direful rage,
Thy crimes have brought, to shorten mortal breath,
With all the numerous family of death.

EVE
My spirits faint, while I these ills foreknow,
And find myself the sad occasion too.
But what is death?

RAPHAEL
In vision thou shalt see his griesly face,
The king of terrors, raging in thy face.
That, while in future fate thou shar'st thy part,
A kind remorse, for sin, may seize thy heart.

[The SCENE shifts, and discovers deaths of several sorts. A Battle at Land, and a Naval Fight.

ADAM
O wretched offspring! O unhappy state
Of all mankind, by me betrayed to fate!
Born, through my crime, to be offenders first;
And, for those sins they could not shun, accurst.

EVE
Why is life forced on man, who, might he chuse,

Would not accept what he with pain must lose?
Unknowing, he receives it; and when, known,
He thinks it his, and values it, 'tis gone.

RAPHAEL
Behold of every age; ripe manhood see,
Decrepid years, and helpless infancy:
Those who, by lingering sickness, lose their breath;
And those who, by despair, suborn their death:
See yon mad fools, who for some trivial right,
For love, or for mistaken honour, fight:
See those, more mad, who throw their lives away
In needless wars; the stakes which monarchs lay,
When for each other's provinces they play.
Then, as if earth too narrow were for fate,
On open seas their quarrels they debate:
In hollow wood they floating armies bear;
And force imprisoned winds to bring them near.

EVE
Who would the miseries of man foreknow?
Not knowing, we but share our part of woe:
Now, we the fate of future ages bear,
And, ere their birth, behold our dead appear.

ADAM
The deaths, thou show'st, are forced and full of strife,
Cast headlong from the precipice of life.
Is there no smooth descent? no painless way
Of kindly mixing with our native clay?

RAPHAEL
There is; but rarely shall that path be trod,
Which, without horror, leads to death's abode.
Some few, by temperance taught, approaching slow,
To distant fate by easy journies go:
Gently they lay them down, as evening sheep
On their own woolly fleeces softly sleep.

ADAM
So noiseless would I live, such death to find;
Like timely fruit, not shaken by the wind,
But ripely dropping from the sapless bough,
And, dying, nothing to myself would owe.

EVE
Thus, daily changing, with a duller taste
Of lessening joys, I, by degrees, would waste:

Still quitting ground, by unperceived decay,
And steal myself from life, and melt away.

RAPHAEL
Death you have seen: Now see your race revive,
How happy they in deathless pleasures live;
Far more than I can show, or you can see,
Shall crown the blest with immortality.

[Here a Heaven descends, full of **ANGELS**, and blessed **SPIRITS**, with soft Music, a Song and Chorus.

ADAM
O goodness infinite! whose heavenly will
Can so much good produce from so much ill!
Happy their state!
Pure, and unchanged, and needing no defence
From sins, as did my frailer innocence.
Their joy sincere, and with no sorrow mixt:
Eternity stands permanent and fixt,
And wheels no longer on the poles of time;
Secure from fate, and more secure from crime.

EVE
Ravished with joy, I can but half repent
The sin, which heaven makes happy in the event.

RAPHAEL
Thus armed, meet firmly your approaching ill;
For see, the guards, from yon' far eastern hill,
Already move, nor longer stay afford;
High in the air they wave the flaming sword,
Your signal to depart; now down amain
They drive, and glide, like meteors, through the plain.

ADAM
Then farewell all; I will indulgent be
To my own ease, and not look back to see.
When what we love we ne'er must meet again,
To lose the thought is to remove the pain.

EVE
Farewell, you happy shades!
Where angels first should practise hymns, and string
Their tuneful harps, when they to heaven would sing.
Farewell, you flowers, whose buds, with early care,
I watched, and to the chearful sun did rear:
Who now shall bind your stems? or, when you fall,
With fountain streams your fainting souls recal?

A long farewell to thee, my nuptial bower,
Adorned with every fair and fragrant flower!
And last, farewell, farewell my place of birth!
I go to wander in the lower earth,
As distant as I can; for, dispossest,
Farthest from what I once enjoyed, is best.

RAPHAEL
The rising winds urge the tempestuous air;
And on their wings deformed winter bear:
The beasts already feel the change; and hence
They fly to deeper coverts, for defence:
The feebler herd before the stronger run;
For now the war of nature is begun:
But, part you hence in peace, and, having mourned your sin,
For outward Eden lost, find Paradise within.

[Exeunt.

John Dryden – A Short Biography

John Dryden was born on August 9th, 1631 in the village rectory of Aldwincle near Thrapston in Northamptonshire, where his maternal grandfather was Rector of All Saints Church.

Dryden was the eldest of fourteen children born to Erasmus Dryden and wife Mary Pickering, paternal grandson of Sir Erasmus Dryden, 1st Baronet (1553–1632) and wife Frances Wilkes, Puritan landowning gentry who supported the Puritan cause and Parliament.

As a boy Dryden lived in the nearby village of Titchmarsh, Northamptonshire where it is probable that he received his first education.

In 1644 he was sent to Westminster School as a King's Scholar where his headmaster was Dr. Richard Busby, a charismatic teacher but severe disciplinarian. Having recently been re-founded by Elizabeth I, Westminster now embraced a very different religious and political spirit encouraging royalism and high Anglicanism but as a humanist public school, it maintained a curriculum which trained pupils in the art of rhetoric and the presentation of arguments for both sides of a given issue. This skill would remain with Dryden and influence his later writing and thinking, as much of it displays these dialectical patterns.

His first published poem, whilst still at Westminster, was an elegy with a strong royalist flavour on the death of his schoolmate Henry, Lord Hastings from smallpox, and alludes to the execution of King Charles I, which took place on January 30th, 1649.

In 1650 Dryden was ready for University and travelled to Trinity College, Cambridge. Dryden's undergraduate years would almost certainly have followed the standard curriculum of classics, rhetoric, and mathematics.

Dryden obtained his BA in 1654, graduating top of the list for Trinity that year.

However family tragedy struck in June of the same year when Dryden's father died, leaving him some land which generated a small income, but not enough to live on.

Returning to London during The Protectorate, Dryden now obtained work with Cromwell's Secretary of State, John Thurloe. This may have been the result of influence exercised on his behalf by his cousin the Lord Chamberlain, Sir Gilbert Pickering.

At Cromwell's funeral on 23 November 1658 Dryden was in the company of the Puritan poets John Milton and Andrew Marvell. The setting was to be a sea change in English history. From Republic to Monarchy and from one set of lauded poets to what would soon become the Age of Dryden.

The start began later that year when Dryden published the first of his great poems, Heroic Stanzas (1658), a eulogy on Cromwell's death which is necessarily cautious and prudent in its emotional display.

With the Restoration of the Monarchy in 1660 Dryden celebrated in verse with Astraea Redux, an authentic royalist panegyric. In this work the interregnum is illustrated as a time of anarchy, and Charles is seen as the restorer of peace and order.

With the king now established Dryden moved quickly to place himself as the leading poet and critic of his day and transferred his allegiances to the new government.

Along with Astraea Redux, Dryden welcomed the new regime with two more panegyrics: To His Sacred Majesty: A Panegyric on his Coronation (1662) and To My Lord Chancellor (1662).

These panegyrics are occasional and written to celebrate events. Thus they are written for the nation rather than the self, but these and others put him in good standing for his eventual appointment as Poet Laureate, where a number of event poems would be required each year and speaking for the Nation and to the Nation would be the first order of duty.

These poems suggest that Dryden was looking to court a possible patron which would have given him an income and time to explore his creative ideas but no, his path instead would be to make a living in writing for publishers, not for the aristocracy, and thus ultimately for the reading public.

In November 1662 Dryden was proposed for membership in the Royal Society, and he was elected an early fellow. However, his inactivity and non payment of dues led to his expulsion in 1666.

On December 1st, 1663 Dryden married the Royalist sister of Sir Robert Howard—Lady Elizabeth Howard (died 1714). The marriage was at St. Swithin's, London, and the consent of the parents is noted on the license, though Lady Elizabeth was then about twenty-five. She was the object of some scandals, well or ill founded; it was said that Dryden had been bullied into the marriage by her brothers. A small estate in Wiltshire was settled upon them by her father. The lady's intellect and temper were apparently not good; her husband was treated as an inferior by those of her social status.

Dryden's works occasionally contain outbursts against the married state but also celebrations of the same. Little else is known of the intimate side of his marriage.

Both Dryden and his wife were warmly attached to their children. They had three sons: Charles (1666–1704), John (1668–1701), and Erasmus Henry (1669–1710). Lady Elizabeth Dryden survived her husband, but went insane soon after his death and died in 1714.

With the re-opening of the theatres after the Puritan ban, Dryden began to also write plays. His first play, The Wild Gallant, appeared in 1663 but was not successful. From 1668 on he was contracted to produce three plays a year for the King's Company, in which he became a shareholder. During the 1660s and '70s, theatrical writing was his main source of income. He led the way in Restoration comedy, his best-known works being Marriage à la Mode (1672), as well as heroic tragedy and regular tragedy, in which his greatest success was All for Love (1678). Dryden was never fully satisfied with his theatrical writings and frequently suggested that his talents were wasted on unworthy audiences.

Certainly therefore fame as a poet looked more rewarding. In 1667, around the same time his dramatic career began, he published Annus Mirabilis, a lengthy historical poem which described the English defeat of the Dutch naval fleet and the Great Fire of London in 1666. It was a modern epic in pentameter quatrains that established him as the pre-eminent poet of his generation, and was crucial in his attaining the posts of Poet Laureate (1668) and then historiographer royal (1670).

When the Great Plague of London closed the theatres in 1665 Dryden retreated to Wiltshire where he wrote Of Dramatick Poesie (1668), arguably the best of his unsystematic prefaces and essays. Dryden constantly defended his own literary practice, and Of Dramatick Poesie, the longest of his critical works, takes the form of a dialogue in which four characters—each based on a prominent contemporary, with Dryden himself as 'Neander'—debate the merits of classical, French and English drama.

He felt strongly about the relation of the poet to tradition and the creative process, and his heroic play Aureng-zebe (1675) has a prologue which denounces the use of rhyme in serious drama. His play All for Love (1678) was written in blank verse, and was to immediately follow Aureng-Zebe.

On December 18th, 1679 he was attacked in Rose Alley near his home in Covent Garden by thugs hired by fellow poet, John Wilmot, 2nd Earl of Rochester, with whom he had a long-standing conflict. Wilmot was constantly in and out of favour with the King and his own poetry was often bawdy, lewd, even obscene and made fun of the King who would often exile him from Court.

Dryden's greatest achievements were in satiric verse: the mock-heroic Mac Flecknoe, a more personal product of his Laureate years, was a lampoon circulated in manuscript and an attack on the playwright Thomas Shadwell. Dryden's main goal in the work is to "satirize Shadwell, ostensibly for his offenses against literature but more immediately we may suppose for his habitual badgering of him on the stage and in print." It is not a belittling form of satire, but rather one which makes his object great in ways which are unexpected, transferring the ridiculous into poetry. This line of satire continued with Absalom and Achitophel (1681) and The Medal (1682). Other major works from this period are the religious poems Religio Laici (1682), written from the position of a member of the Church of England; his 1683 edition of Plutarch's Lives, translated From the Greek by Several Hands in which he introduced the word biography to English readers; and The Hind and the Panther, (1687) which celebrates his conversion to Roman Catholicism.

He wrote Britannia Rediviva celebrating the birth of a son and heir to the Catholic King and Queen on June 10th, 1688. When later in the same year James II was deposed in the Glorious Revolution, Dryden's refusal to take the oaths of allegiance to the new monarchs, William and Mary, which left him out of favour at court and he had to leave his post as Poet Laureate. Thomas Shadwell, his despised rival, succeeded him. Dryden, England's greatest literary figure, was now forced to give up his public offices and live by the proceeds of his pen alone.

Dryden was an excellent translator with his own style which brought the ire of many critics. Many felt he would embellish or expand anything he felt short or curt. Dryden did not feel such expansion was a fault, arguing that as Latin is a naturally concise language it cannot be duly represented by a comparable number of words in the much larger English vocabulary. He continued with his task of translating works by Horace, Juvenal, Ovid, Lucretius, and Theocritus, a task which he found far more satisfying than writing for the stage.

In 1694 he began work on what would be his most ambitious and defining work as translator, The Works of Virgil (1697), which was published by subscription. The publication of the translation of Virgil was a national event and brought Dryden the sum of £1,400.

His final translations appeared in the volume Fables Ancient and Modern (1700), a series of episodes from Homer, Ovid, and Boccaccio, as well as modernised adaptations from Geoffrey Chaucer interspersed with Dryden's own poems. As a translator, he made great literary works in the older languages available to readers of English.

John Dryden died on May 12th, 1700, and was initially buried in St. Anne's cemetery in Soho, before being exhumed and reburied in Westminster Abbey ten days later. He was the subject of poetic eulogies, such as Luctus Brittannici: or the Tears of the British Muses; for the Death of John Dryden, Esq. (London, 1700), and The Nine Muses.

He is seen as dominating the literary life of Restoration England to such a point that the period came to be known in literary circles as the Age of Dryden. Walter Scott called him "Glorious John."

Dryden was the dominant literary figure and influence of his age. He established the heroic couplet as a standard form of English poetry by writing successful satires, religious pieces, fables, epigrams, compliments, prologues, and plays with it; he also introduced the alexandrine and triplet into the form. In his poems, translations, and criticism, he established a poetic diction appropriate to the heroic couplet—Auden referred to him as "the master of the middle style"—that was a model for his contemporaries and for much of the 18th century. The considerable loss felt by the English literary community at his death was evident in the elegies written about him. Dryden's heroic couplet went on to become the dominant poetic form of the 18th century.

What Dryden achieved in his poetry was neither the emotional excitement of the early nineteenth-century romantics nor the intellectual complexities of the metaphysicals. Although he uses formal structures such as heroic couplets, he tried to recreate the natural rhythm of speech, and he knew that different subjects need different kinds of verse. In his preface to Religio Laici he says that "the expressions of a poem designed purely for instruction ought to be plain and natural, yet majestic... The florid, elevated and figurative way is for the passions; for (these) are begotten in the soul by showing the objects out of their true proportion.... A man is to be cheated into passion, but to be reasoned into truth."

Perhaps the following illustrates Dryden and his life—"The way I have taken, is not so streight as Metaphrase, nor so loose as Paraphrase: Some things too I have omitted, and sometimes added of my own. Yet the omissions I hope, are but of Circumstances, and such as wou'd have no grace in English; and the Addition, I also hope, are easily deduc'd from Virgil's Sense. They will seem (at least I have the Vanity to think so), not struck into him, but growing out of him".

John Dryden – A Concise Bibliography

Astraea Redux, 1660
The Wild Gallant (comedy), 1663
The Indian Emperour (tragedy), 1665
Annus Mirabilis (poem), 1667
The Enchanted Island (comedy), 1667, with William D'Avenant from Shakespeare's The Tempest
Secret Love, or The Maiden Queen, 1667
An Essay of Dramatick Poesie, 1668
An Evening's Love (comedy), 1668
Tyrannick Love (tragedy), 1669
The Conquest of Granada, 1670
The Assignation, or Love in a Nunnery, 1672
Marriage à la mode, 1672
Amboyna, or the Cruelties of the Dutch to the English Merchants, 1673
The Mistaken Husband (comedy), 1674
Aureng-zebe, 1675
All for Love, 1678
Oedipus (heroic drama), 1679, an adaptation with Nathaniel Lee of Sophocles' Oedipus
Absalom and Achitophel, 1681
The Spanish Fryar, 1681
Mac Flecknoe, 1682
The Medal, 1682
Religio Laici, 1682
To the Memory of Mr. Oldham, 1684
Threnodia Augustalis, 1685
The Hind and the Panther, 1687
A Song for St. Cecilia's Day, 1687
Britannia Rediviva, 1688, written to mark the birth of a Prince of Wales.
Amphitryon, 1690
Don Sebastian (play), 1690
Creator Spirit, by whose aid, 1690. Translation of Rabanus Maurus' Veni Creator Spiritus
King Arthur, 1691
Cleomenes, 1692
The Art of Satire, 1693
Love Triumphant, 1694
The Works of Virgil, 1697
Alexander's Feast, 1697
Fables, Ancient and Modern, 1700

www.ingramcontent.com/pod-product-compliance
Lightning Source LLC
Chambersburg PA
CBHW061511040426
42450CB00008B/1567